UKRAINE HISTORY

*A Comprehensive Look at
Ukraine's Rich & Complex
History of Empires,
Nationalism, War, & Political
Strife*

HISTORY BROUGHT ALIVE

FREE BONUS FROM HBA: EBOOK BUNDLE

Greetings!

First of all, thank you for reading our books. As fellow passionate readers of History and Mythology, we aim to create the very best books for our readers.

Now, we invite you to join our VIP list. As a welcome gift, we offer the History & Mythology Ebook Bundle below for free. Plus you can be the first to receive new books and exclusives! <u>Remember it's 100% free to join.</u>

Simply scan the QR code to join.

Keep up to date with us on:

YouTube: History Brought Alive

Facebook: History Brought Alive

www.historybroughtalive.com

CONTENTS

INTRODUCTION

As a country that has been at the crossroads of major historical events, Ukraine has a rich and complex history that spans centuries. From the Kievan Rus' period to the modern-day conflict with Russia, Ukrainian history is filled with stories of kings and queens, revolutions and wars, and the struggles of a people to maintain their unique identity. Ukrainian history is filled with stories of heroism, tragedy, and triumph. From the early days of the Kievan Rus' to the present-day conflict with Russia, Ukrainian history is a testament to the resilience of the Ukrainian people. The history continues to shape the country's political and social landscape. By learning about Ukrainian history, people can better understand the challenges that Ukraine faces today, and promote tolerance and understanding between different cultures.

Importance and Relevance of Ukrainian History

Studying Ukrainian history is crucial for understanding the country's culture, traditions, and identity. Ukraine has a long and complex history that has shaped the country's current political, economic, and social situation. Without an understanding of Ukrainian history, it is impossible to comprehend the challenges that Ukraine faces today.

Another good thing about studying Ukrainian history is that it helps to challenge stereotypes and misconceptions about the country. For example, many people still believe that Ukraine is a part of Russia, or that Ukrainian culture is similar to Russian culture. However, by studying Ukrainian history, it becomes clear that Ukraine has a unique culture, language, and history that is distinct from Russia.

Moreover, studying Ukrainian history helps to promote tolerance and understanding between different cultures. By learning about the struggles and triumphs of the Ukrainian people, we can better understand their perspectives and experiences. This, in turn, can help to break down barriers between different cultures and promote a more peaceful and inclusive world.

One of the defining features of Ukrainian history is the country's struggle for independence. For centuries, Ukraine was ruled by foreign powers, including the Mongols, Poles, Lithuanians, Austrians, and Russians. However, throughout this period, the Ukrainian people maintained their distinct identity and fought for their right to self-determination.

Another defining feature of Ukrainian history is the country's rich cultural heritage. Ukraine is home to numerous cultural traditions, including music, dance, literature, and art. Many of these traditions have been preserved through the centuries and continue to be celebrated today.

The impact of Ukrainian history on modern Ukraine is profound. The country's struggle for independence and its rich cultural heritage continue to shape the country's identity and political landscape. One of the most significant events in modern Ukrainian history is the 2014 Revolution of Dignity. This was a popular uprising that overthrew the corrupt and authoritarian government of Viktor Yanukovych, and paved the way for a more democratic and inclusive Ukraine. The Revolution of Dignity was a defining moment in

Ukrainian history, and it demonstrated the power of the Ukrainian people to effect change.

Another important aspect of modern Ukrainian history is the ongoing conflict with Russia. Since 2014, Russia has annexed Crimea and supported separatist movements in eastern Ukraine. This conflict has had a profound impact on the country, causing a humanitarian crisis and dividing the Ukrainian people.

Major Periods and Events in Ukrainian History

Ukrainian history has also been shaped by global events. Throughout its history, Ukraine has been at the crossroads of major historical events, including wars, revolutions, and political upheavals. One of the most significant global events in Ukrainian history was World War II. During the war, Ukraine was occupied by the Nazis, who committed numerous atrocities against the Ukrainian people. This period of Ukrainian history is known as the "Holocaust by Bullets", and it resulted in the deaths of millions of Ukrainians. Another significant global event in Ukrainian history was the collapse of the Soviet Union. Ukraine was one of the republics that declared independence from the Soviet Union in 1991, and this event paved the way for a more democratic and independent Ukraine.

Here is a look at some of the major events that shaped the political landscape, the history, and the identity of Ukraine as a country:

- The establishment of the Kievan Rus' in the 9th century

The 9th century saw the emergence of a powerful and influential state in Eastern Europe known as the Kievan Rus'. This state was established by the Varangians, a group of Scandinavian warriors who settled in the region and forged alliances with the local Slavic tribes. With their military prowess and strategic alliances, the Varangians were able to unite the disparate tribes of the region under a single banner and establish a powerful state that would endure for centuries. The Kievan Rus' was not only a political and military power but also a center of culture and learning, with a rich tradition of art, literature, and architecture. Its legacy can still be felt today in the customs, language, and culture of modern-day Russia, Ukraine, and Belarus.

- The Mongol invasion of Ukraine in the 13th century

The Mongol invasion of Ukraine in the 13th century was a pivotal moment in the region's history. This brutal campaign saw the Mongol Empire under the leadership of Batu Khan, the grandson of Genghis Khan, sweep across Eastern Europe, leaving a trail of destruction in their wake. The invasion had a profound impact on the people of Ukraine, forever altering the political and social landscape of the region. With their superior military tactics and weaponry, the Mongols were able to conquer cities and towns, leaving them in ruins and decimating the local population. Despite the devastating consequences of the invasion, it also led to significant cultural exchanges between the Mongols and the people of Ukraine, as well as the spread of new technologies and ideas.

- The Union of Lublin in 1569, which united Poland and Ukraine

The Union of Lublin in 1569 was a historic event that marked the unification of two powerful kingdoms, Poland and Lithuania. This union was a landmark achievement that brought together two distinct cultures, languages, and religions to create a powerful force that shaped the future of Eastern Europe. The Union of Lublin was the result of years of negotiations and diplomatic efforts between the two nations, and it paved the way for the emergence of a new political entity that was destined to become a major player on the European stage. The impact of this union was felt far beyond its borders, and it set a precedent for other nations to follow in the centuries that followed. This event was a defining moment in the history of Poland and Lithuania, and it continues to be celebrated as a symbol of unity and strength to this day.

- The Khmelnytsky Uprising in the 17th century, which sought to liberate Ukraine from Polish rule

The Khmelnytsky Uprising of the 17th century was one of the most significant events in Eastern European history. It marked a turning point in the struggle for independence and freedom from foreign domination, and it ultimately paved the way for the formation of the modern Ukrainian state. The uprising was led by Bohdan Khmelnytsky, a charismatic and courageous leader who rallied his people against the oppressive rule of the Polish-Lithuanian Commonwealth. With a small army of Cossacks and peasants, Khmelnytsky defeated the Polish forces in a series of decisive battles, securing the autonomy and self-determination of the Ukrainian people. The legacy of the Khmelnytsky Uprising still resonates today, and it serves as a reminder of the power of collective action and the resilience of the human spirit in the face of oppression.

- The annexation of Ukraine by the Russian Empire in the 18th century

The annexation of Ukraine by the Russian Empire in the 18th century is a topic that has sparked much controversy and debate over the years. For centuries, Ukraine had been a territory that was constantly fought over by various powers, including Poland, Turkey, and Russia. However, it was the Russian Empire that ultimately succeeded in annexing Ukraine in the late 18th century. This event marked a significant turning point in the history of Ukraine and had far-reaching consequences that are still felt today. Some argue that the annexation was necessary for Russia's expansion and security, while others see it as an act of aggression and imperialism. Regardless of one's perspective, the annexation of Ukraine remains an important historical event that has shaped the politics and culture of the region for centuries to come.

- The Ukrainian War of Independence in 1917-1921, which established the short-lived Ukrainian People's Republic

The Ukrainian War of Independence, also

known as the Ukrainian Revolution, was a series of conflicts that took place between 1917 and 1921. This struggle for freedom was fought against the backdrop of World War I and the Russian Revolution, which provided a unique opportunity for Ukrainians to fight for their independence. The Ukrainian people had long been oppressed by foreign powers, including the Austro-Hungarian Empire and the Russian Empire, and the war of independence was their chance to finally break free from the shackles of oppression. The conflict was marked by fierce fighting, political intrigue, and shifting alliances, and it ultimately resulted in the establishment of the Ukrainian Soviet Socialist Republic. Despite the challenges and hardships faced by the Ukrainian people during this time, their struggle for independence remains a powerful symbol of resilience and determination.

- The Holodomor famine in 1932-1933, which killed millions of Ukrainians

The Holodomor famine of 1932-1933 is one of the most tragic and devastating events in human history. It was a man-made famine that occurred in Soviet Ukraine, resulting in the deaths of millions of people. The Holodomor is often referred to as a genocide, as it was a deliberate act of starvation and extermination by the Soviet government. The famine was brought on by a combination of factors, including collectivization policies, forced grain requisitions, and government mismanagement. The Holodomor was not widely known outside of the Soviet Union until decades later, and it remains a controversial topic to this day. Despite the attempts to cover up the tragedy, the legacy and impact of the Holodomor continue to be felt by the Ukrainian people and the world.

- The Chernobyl disaster in 1986, which had a profound impact on the country's environment and health

In 1986, the world was shaken by one of the worst nuclear disasters in history–the Chernobyl disaster. It happened in Pripyat, a small city in the north of the Ukrainian SSR, and it left a lasting impact on the environment, the people, and the world as a whole. The incident occurred when a reactor at the Chernobyl nuclear power plant exploded, releasing large amounts of radioactive material into the atmosphere. The result was tragic, with many people being exposed to dangerous levels of radiation, and the surrounding area being contaminated for decades to come. The aftermath of the disaster has been widely documented, and it remains a haunting reminder of the importance of safety and responsibility in nuclear energy.

- The 2014 Revolution of Dignity, which overthrew the corrupt government of Viktor Yanukovych

In 2014, the Ukrainian Revolution of Dignity shook the world and captured the attention of millions. It was a time of political and social upheaval as protestors took to the streets to demand change and a better future for their country. The revolution was sparked by the decision of then-President Viktor Yanukovych to reject a trade deal with the European Union in favor of closer ties with Russia. This decision was met with outrage from Ukrainians who saw it as a betrayal of their aspirations for a closer relationship with the West. The protests that followed were some of the largest in Ukraine's history, with demonstrators occupying the streets of Kiev for months. The Revolution of Dignity ultimately succeeded in ousting Yanukovych from power and ushering in a new era of democracy and reform in Ukraine. This momentous event continues to be remembered and celebrated by Ukrainians and serves as a reminder of the power of collective action and the human desire for freedom and justice.

Ukrainian history is also filled with key figures who have shaped the country's identity and political landscape. Some of the most important figures include:

- Volodymyr the Great, who established Christianity in the Kievan Rus'
- Taras Shevchenko, a renowned poet and writer who played a key role in the Ukrainian national revival
- Ivan Mazepa, a Ukrainian nobleman who led a rebellion against the Russian Empire in the 18th century
- Mykhailo Hrushevsky, a historian and politician who played a key role in the Ukrainian War of Independence
- Stepan Bandera, a nationalist leader who fought for Ukrainian independence during World War II
- Viktor Yushchenko, a former president of Ukraine who played a key role in the Orange Revolution of 2004
- Petro Poroshenko, a former president of Ukraine who played a key role in the country's fight against Russian aggression

Resources for Learning about Ukrainian History

There are many resources available for those

who wish to learn more about Ukrainian history. Some of the best resources include:

Books: There are many books available on Ukrainian history, ranging from academic texts to popular histories. Some of the most popular books include "A History of Ukraine" by Paul Robert Magocsi and "Bloodlands: Europe between Hitler and Stalin" by Timothy Snyder.

Museums: There are many museums in Ukraine that focus on the country's history and culture. Some of the most popular museums include the National Museum of Ukrainian History and the Museum of the History of Ukraine in World War II.

Online Resources: There are many online resources available for those who wish to learn more about Ukrainian history. Some of the best resources include the Ukrainian Institute of National Memory and the Ukrainian History and Education Center.

CHAPTER 1
ANCIENT UKRAINE (PRE-9ᵀᴴ CENTURY)

———————— ⚜ ————————

The history of Kievan Rus" is a fascinating topic that has fascinated scholars and enthusiasts for centuries. One of the key influences on the formation of this medieval state was the Scythian and Sarmatian cultures. These nomadic tribes lived in the region that is now Ukraine and Russia during the early medieval period, and their impact on the culture and society of Kievan Rus" was significant. From their distinctive art and architecture to their military tactics and social organization, the Scythians and Sarmatians left an indelible mark on the early history of this important region. This chapter will explore the influence of the ancient cultures on Kievan Rus" and examine the ways in which they shaped the development of the medieval state and contributed to its unique character and identity.

Overview of the Early Slavic Tribes in the Region

Ancient Ukraine was inhabited by various Slavic tribes from the 6th century onwards. These tribes played a major role in the history of Ukraine and their legacy can still be seen today. The most prominent of these tribes were the Drevlians, Krivichs, Radimichs, Severians, and Viatichi. These Slavic tribes had a significant impact on Ukrainian culture and language as well as its economic development. They also left behind many archaeological sites that are still being studied today. The influence of these ancient Slavic tribes is still felt in modern day Ukraine, and they remain an important part of its heritage and identity.

The Drevlians left behind a significant archaeological site at the ancient fortress of Yativka in Ukraine. This site was first discovered and excavated by Soviet archaeologists in 1960, and it is now designated as an archaeological monument. The Drevlians inhabited the eastern and southern parts of Ukraine, particularly around present day Chernivtsi and Drohobych cities. They were one of the earliest groups to settle in the region which still bears their name today—Drah Vlah meaning 'land for Scythian' or 'land for invaders' according to different translations. The Drevlians left behind a significant archaeological site at the ancient fortress of Yativka in Ukraine. This site was first discovered and excavated by Soviet archaeologists in 1960 and it is now designated as an archaeological monument. The Drevlians were an Indo-European people who are believed to have migrated from the North Caucasus and settled in Ukraine around 3000 BC. They were a warrior society, which was eventually superseded by the Slavs and other Indo-European groups.

The Drevlians occupied vast swathes of land from their base in present day Ukraine to present day Moldova, including parts of modern Romania, Bulgaria and Hungary. Their territory also included parts of what is now southern Poland and western Russia, although it shrank significantly due to expansion of the Scythians led by Ptolemy II Philadelphus, who conquered the Drevlians in around 250 BC. The Drevlians were one of three major "barbarian" nations along with the Cimmerians and the Scythians. The Drevlians spoke a North Caucasian language known as "Druvilo" or "Druvle".

The Drevlians were one of the first people to adopt bronze weapons and the horse-drawn war chariot, which they used militarily in conjunction with their cavalry. They began to dominate areas around modern-day Poland, Hungary, and Bulgaria by 800 BC. They led many incursions into Europe as far as Greece, although they were unable to maintain these conquests. A barbarian people is a social group that is perceived as uncivilized or primitive because of its distant cultural traditions. The term is usually used pejoratively; however, some argue that it may also be used in a complimentary sense, as an acknowledgment of cultural diversity.

The term 'barbarism' may also refer to the Barbarian invasions. The word "barbarian" comes from Greek barbaros (βαρβαρος), translated as foreign-speaking or non-Greek. The root word barbara (βάρβαρος), which also gave us the English word "barbaric", means "of, relating to, or spoken by" non-Greeks in ancient Greek. Thus, like many other words with similar meanings such as "Babylonian", barbaros does not imply that the science was any less advanced than that of Greece.

The term is often used as a pejorative, as in barbaric cultures, which refer to more than one person or to denigrate others. In ancient times, the term "barbarian" was not generally used to refer to people who were outside the political-cultural norms of a society, instead it referred primarily to those who were beyond the ancient borders of the civilization in question. A barbarian might have been understood as a person that was from outside nations or tribes or that spoke an unknown language. While barbarians were previously excluded from civilized life by culture and race, with time, it became possible for any individual to be considered "barbarian" when they were perceived as not behaving like a member of the culture in which they were living.

Impact of Scythian and Sarmatian Cultures

The vast Eurasian plains have been home to many nomadic tribes throughout history, but few have left a lasting impact like the Scythians and Sarmatians. These two groups were known for their horsemanship, warrior skills, and unique culture and beliefs. Today, their legacy lives on through archaeological discoveries, ancient texts, and even modern-day descendants. In this article, we will explore the fascinating world of the Scythians and Sarmatians and their impact on history.

The Scythians and Sarmatians were nomadic tribes that roamed the Eurasian steppes from the 8th century BCE to the 4th century CE. They lived in the region that is now Ukraine and

Russia during the early medieval period. They were skilled horse riders and hunters who lived in portable dwellings made of felt and animal skins. These tribes were known for their distinctive art and architecture, military tactics, and social organization, all of which had a significant impact on the culture and society of Kievan Rus'. They were also known for their ability to adapt to the harsh conditions of the steppes. One of the most notable ways in which the Scythians and Sarmatians influenced Kievan Rus' was through their art, which was characterized by intricate designs and patterns that were often incorporated into clothing, jewelry, and other decorative objects.

The Scythians were the first to emerge on the scene, with their origins dating back to the 8th century BCE. They were made up of several different tribes, united by their nomadic lifestyle and their language, which belonged to the Iranian branch of the Indo-European family. The Scythians were a powerful force in the region for centuries, and their influence spread as far as the Black Sea, the Caucasus, and Central Asia.

The Sarmatians, on the other hand, emerged later, around the 5th century BCE. They were also a nomadic tribe, but their language and culture were different from the Scythians. The Sarmatians spoke a language that belonged to the Eastern Iranian branch of the Indo-European family, and their culture was heavily influenced by the Scythians. They were known for their skilled horsemanship and their fierce warrior culture.

The Scythians and Sarmatians had a rich culture and unique beliefs that set them apart from other nomadic tribes of the time. They were skilled artisans who created intricate gold jewelry, weapons, and other objects that have been found in archaeological digs. Their art was highly stylized and often depicted scenes from their daily lives, such as hunting, warfare, and feasting.

The Scythians and Sarmatians also had a complex religion, which involved the worship of several gods and goddesses. One of the most important deities was the sky god, who was believed to control the weather and the seasons. Other gods included a fertility goddess, a war god, and a death god. The Scythians and Sarmatians also believed in an afterlife, which they believed was a paradise-like realm where they would be reunited with their ancestors.

The Scythians and Sarmatians were home to many famous figures throughout history. One of the most famous Scythians was Queen Tomyris, who ruled over the Massagetae tribe in the 6th century BCE. She is known for her victory over the Persian king Cyrus the Great, who tried to invade her kingdom.

Another famous Scythian was the warrior prince Spargapises, who led a rebellion against the Persian king Darius I in the 5th century BCE. He was ultimately captured and executed, but his bravery inspired other Scythians to rebel against Persian rule. As for the Sarmatians, one of the most famous figures was the warrior queen Tomris, who ruled over the Sarmatian tribe in the 3rd century BCE. She is known for her victory over the Macedonian general Seleucus I, who tried to invade her kingdom.

The Scythians and Sarmatians had a significant impact on the history of the Eurasian steppes and beyond. They were skilled warriors who were feared by their enemies and admired by their allies. They were also skilled traders who established trade routes that connected the East and the West.

One of the most significant contributions of the Scythians and Sarmatians was their impact on the Greek world. The Greeks referred to the Scythians as "barbarians", but they also recognized their power and influence. The

Scythians and Sarmatians played a significant role in the Greek-Persian wars, and their warriors were even hired as mercenaries by the Greeks.

The Scythians and Sarmatians also had an impact on the Roman Empire. The Romans encountered the Sarmatians in the 1st century CE, and they were impressed by their warrior skills and their unique culture. The Romans even adopted some aspects of Sarmatian culture, such as their cavalry tactics.

Archaeological evidence of Scythian and Sarmatian influence in Kievan Rus' can be seen in the numerous burial mounds and other artifacts that have been discovered in the region. These artifacts include weapons, jewelry, and other decorative objects that feature Scythian and Sarmatian designs and motifs. In addition, many of the architectural features of Kievan Rus' buildings, such as the use of wooden beams and the construction of defensive walls, were influenced by the military tactics and engineering skills of the Scythians and Sarmatians.

The Scythians and Sarmatians played a significant role in the formation of Kievan Rus' by contributing to the development of its culture, economy, and military strength. The nomadic lifestyle of these tribes, which involved constant movement and adaptation to changing environments, helped to shape the social organization and economic practices of Kievan Rus'. In addition, the military tactics and engineering skills of the Scythians and Sarmatians were instrumental in the defense and expansion of Kievan Rus".

The legacy of Scythian and Sarmatian cultures can still be seen in modern-day Ukraine, where many of the art and architectural traditions of these ancient tribes continue to influence contemporary design and aesthetics. In addition, the nomadic lifestyle and cultural practices of the Scythians and Sarmatians have also had an impact on the development of Ukrainian society and culture, particularly in rural areas where traditional practices are still observed.

The Scythians and Sarmatians may be long gone, but their legacy lives on through their unique culture and beliefs. Their impact on history cannot be understated, as they played a significant role in the development of the Eurasian steppes and their interactions with neighboring civilizations. Today, their legacy lives on through archaeological discoveries, ancient texts, and even modern-day descendants. The Scythians and Sarmatians were truly remarkable nomadic tribes that will always be remembered as a part of history.

Emergence of Kievan Rus"

Kievan Rus' was a medieval state that emerged in the late 9th century in what is now Ukraine and Russia. The state was founded by the East Slavic tribes, who were united under the leadership of the Viking warrior, Rurik. The early history of Kievan Rus' was marked by political instability and conflict, as various factions vied for power and influence. However, by the 10th century, the state had established itself as a major power in Eastern Europe and had developed a distinct culture and identity that was influenced by a variety of factors, including the Scythian and Sarmatian cultures.

CHAPTER 2
KIEVAN RUS

The medieval state of Kievan Rus' is a fascinating and important part of Eastern European history. This ancient empire, which existed from the 9th to the 13th centuries, was a powerful force that shaped the development of modern-day Russia and Ukraine. From its capital city of Kiev, Kievan Rus' was renowned for its sophisticated culture, impressive architecture, and formidable military might. Today, the legacy of Kievan Rus' can be seen in the art, literature, and traditions of both Russia and Ukraine.

The Establishment and Growth of Kievan Rus"

The origins of Kievan Rus' can be traced back to the 9th century, when a group of Slavic tribes banded together to form a loose confederation. This confederation was centered around the city of Kiev, which would later become the capital of Kievan Rus'. In the 10th century, Kievan Rus' began to expand its territory, conquering neighboring tribes and establishing trade relationships with Byzantium and the Arab world.

Kievan Rus' was ruled by a series of powerful princes, who wielded both political and military power. The most famous of these princes was Vlodomyr the Great, who converted to Christianity in 988 and made it the official religion of Kievan Rus'. This conversion helped to cement Kievan Rus''s place as a major player in the Eastern European political and cultural scene.

Kievan Rus' continued to thrive throughout the 11th and 12th centuries, with Kiev becoming a major center of trade and culture. However, the empire began to decline in the 13th century, as it was beset by internal strife and external attacks from Mongol invaders. By the end of the 13th century, Kievan Rus' had ceased to exist as a unified state.

The Mongol Invasion and its Impact on Ukraine

The Mongol invasion of Ukraine in the 13th century was a pivotal moment in the region's history. The Mongols, led by the notorious Genghis Khan, swept through Ukraine, leaving behind a trail of destruction and political upheaval. The Mongol conquest had a profound impact on Ukraine's political and social landscape, shaping the region's future for centuries to come. In this article, we will explore the consequences of the Mongol invasion on Ukraine, examining how it altered the country's political and social structures, and how it ultimately led to the emergence of a new order in the region. From the rise of the Mongol Empire to the establishment of the Golden Horde, we will delve into the fascinating history of Ukraine's encounter with the Mongols, and the legacy that it left behind. So, join us on this journey back in time, as we explore the impact of the Mongol invasion on Ukraine's political and social landscape.

Before the Mongol invasion, Ukraine was a land of various principalities that were in constant conflict with each other. The region was divided into different territories, each ruled by a prince, who was in charge of collecting taxes and maintaining law and order. The princes were often at odds with each other, and wars were commonplace. Ukraine was also a battleground for different empires, including the Byzantine, the Kievan Rus', and the Polish-Lithuanian Commonwealth.

The political landscape of Ukraine before the Mongol invasion was characterized by a lack of unity and political instability (Cartwright, 2019). The princes were constantly vying for power, and alliances were often short-lived. The region was in dire need of a strong leader who could unite the different principalities and bring stability to the region. However, this was not to be, as the Mongol invasion would change the political landscape of Ukraine forever.

In 1237, the Mongols, led by Batu Khan, invaded Ukraine. The Mongols were a formidable force, and their conquest of Ukraine was swift and brutal. The Mongols destroyed many of the cities and towns they encountered, and the population was decimated. The Mongols were also successful in subjugating the various principalities and bringing them under their control.

The Mongol invasion had a profound impact on Ukraine's political landscape. The Mongols established the Golden Horde, a Mongol khanate that ruled over Ukraine and other regions of Eastern Europe. The Golden Horde was ruled by a Khan, who was responsible for maintaining law and order, collecting taxes, and waging war. The Khan was also responsible for appointing local rulers, who were in charge of governing their respective territories.

Under the Golden Horde, Ukraine was no longer a collection of independent principalities. Instead, it was a unified region, governed by a central authority. The Mongols brought stability to the region, and the various principalities were no longer at war with each other. However, the Golden Horde was also a foreign power, and the people of Ukraine were forced to pay tribute to the Mongol Khan. The Mongols also imposed their own language and culture on the region, which had a lasting impact on Ukrainian culture.

As mentioned before, prior to the Mongol invasion, Ukraine was a land of various ethnic groups, including Slavs, Greeks, and Tatars. The region was also home to a significant Jewish population, who were often persecuted by the ruling princes (Cartwright, 2019). The social landscape of Ukraine was characterized by a strict hierarchy, with the ruling princes at the top, followed by the nobles, and then the common people.

The people of Ukraine were also deeply religious, with Christianity being the dominant religion. Ukraine was home to many monasteries and churches, which served as centers of learning and culture. The people of Ukraine were also skilled craftsmen, and they produced a range of goods, including pottery, textiles, and metalwork.

The Mongol invasion had a profound impact

on Ukraine's social landscape. The Mongols destroyed many of the cities and towns they encountered, and the population was decimated. The Mongols also brought their own culture and traditions to the region, which had a lasting impact on Ukrainian culture. Under the Golden Horde, the social hierarchy of Ukraine was also transformed. The ruling princes were replaced by Mongol governors, who were often from different ethnic groups. The nobles were also replaced by a new class of people, who were loyal to the Mongol Khan. The common people were also affected by the Mongol invasion, as they were forced to pay tribute to the Mongol Khan.

The Mongol invasion also had an impact on religion in Ukraine. While the Mongols were not particularly religious, they allowed the people of Ukraine to practice their own religion. However, the Mongols also brought their own religious beliefs to the region, which had a lasting impact on Ukrainian culture. The Mongols introduced Islam to Ukraine, and many people converted to the new religion.

The Mongol invasion led to significant cultural changes in Ukraine. The Mongols brought their own language and culture to the region, which had a lasting impact on Ukrainian culture. The Mongols also introduced new technologies and techniques to the region, including gunpowder and siege warfare. Under the Golden Horde, Ukraine became a center of trade and commerce. The Mongols established trade routes that linked Ukraine with other regions of the world, including China and Europe.

The people of Ukraine also traded with each other, exchanging goods and ideas. This led to the emergence of a new culture in Ukraine, which was a fusion of different ethnic groups and traditions. The Mongol invasion also had an impact on Ukrainian literature and art. The Mongols introduced new forms of literature and art to the region, including epic poetry and miniature art. The people of Ukraine also created their own literature and art, which was influenced by Mongol culture. The Mongol invasion led to the emergence of a new cultural identity in Ukraine, which was a fusion of different traditions and influences.

The Mongol invasion had a lasting impact on Ukraine. The Golden Horde ruled over Ukraine for centuries, and the region was never the same again. The Mongol invasion transformed Ukraine from a collection of independent principalities to a unified region, governed by a central authority. The Mongols brought stability to the region, but they also imposed their own culture and traditions on the people of Ukraine. The Mongol invasion also had an impact on Ukrainian culture, literature, and art. The Mongols introduced new forms of literature and art to the region, which had a lasting impact on Ukrainian culture. The Mongol invasion also led to the emergence of a new cultural identity in Ukraine, which was a fusion of different traditions and influences.

The Mongol invasion had a significant impact on many regions of the world, including China, Russia, and the Middle East. The impact of the Mongol invasion varied from region to region, depending on a range of factors, including the political and social structures of the region, and the extent of the Mongol conquest.

In China, for example, the Mongol invasion led to the establishment of the Yuan Dynasty, which ruled over China for several centuries. The Mongol invasion also had an impact on Chinese culture, literature, and art. In Russia, the Mongol invasion led to the establishment of the Golden Horde, which ruled over Russia for several centuries. The Mongol invasion also had an impact on Russian culture, literature, and art.

The impact of the Mongol invasion on Ukraine was significant, but it was also different from the impact on other regions. The Mongol invasion transformed Ukraine from a collection of independent principalities to a unified region, governed by a central authority. The Mongols brought stability to the region, but they also imposed their own culture and traditions on the people of Ukraine. The Mongol invasion also had an impact on Ukrainian culture, literature, and art, leading to the emergence of a new cultural identity in Ukraine.

The legacy of the Mongol invasion can still be felt in Ukraine today, and the impact of the Mongol invasion on Ukraine continues to be studied and celebrated. The Mongol invasion was a pivotal moment in Ukraine's history, and it continues to fascinate historians and scholars around the world.

The Cultural, Political, and Economic Achievements of the Decline and Collapse of Kievan Rus"

Kievan Rus' was a complex and sophisticated society, with a hierarchical social structure that was based on both birth and wealth. At the top of the social ladder were the princes and their families, who held the most political and economic power. Below them were the boyars, or nobles, who were wealthy landowners and held important positions in the government. The majority of the population were peasants, who worked the land and paid taxes to the ruling class.

Kievan Rus' was also home to a vibrant culture, with a rich tradition of art, music, and literature. The most famous example of Kievan Rus' art is the onion-domed architecture that can still be seen in many Eastern European cities today. This architecture is characterized by its distinctive bulbous domes, which were often painted in bright colors and adorned with intricate patterns.

Kievan Rus' literature was also a major cultural force, with the most famous work being the Primary Chronicle. This chronicle, which was compiled in the 12th century, is a detailed account of the history of Kievan Rus', and is still studied by historians today. Other notable works of Kievan Rus' literature include epic poems like The Tale of Igor's Campaign, which tells the story of a prince's failed attempt to conquer a neighboring tribe.

Kievan Rus' architecture and art were some of the most sophisticated and impressive in the medieval world. The most famous example of

Kievan Rus' architecture is the Kiev Pechersk Lavra, a complex of churches and monasteries that was founded in the 11th century. This complex is known for its stunning frescoes, intricate mosaics, and impressive gold leaf work.

Another example of Kievan Rus' architecture is the St. Sophia Cathedral in Kiev, which was built in the 11th century and is now a UNESCO World Heritage Site. This cathedral is known for its impressive frescoes, which depict scenes from the Bible and the lives of the saints. Kievan Rus' art was also a major cultural force, with the most famous examples being the icons that were produced in Kievan Rus' churches. These icons were typically painted on wood, and depicted religious figures like Jesus, Mary, and the saints. Kievan Rus' icons were known for their intricate detail and bright colors, and were often used as objects of veneration by the faithful.

The legacy of Kievan Rus' can still be seen in the culture and traditions of modern Russia and Ukraine. One of the most obvious examples of this influence is the onion-domed architecture that can be found in many Eastern European cities. This architecture is a direct descendant of the Kievan Rus' style, and is a testament to the enduring legacy of this medieval state.

Despite its many achievements, Kievan Rus' was ultimately brought down by a combination of internal strife and external attacks. In the 13th century, the Mongols invaded Kievan Rus' and conquered much of its territory. This invasion plunged Kievan Rus' into a period of decline from which it would never recover. By the end of the 13th century, Kievan Rus' had ceased to exist as a unified state, and its territory was divided among a number of smaller principalities. These principalities would go on to become the foundation of modern-day Russia and Ukraine, but the legacy of Kievan Rus' continued to be felt throughout the region.

Kievan Rus' had a profound influence on the literature and language of Russia and Ukraine. Many of the words and phrases used in these languages today can be traced back to Old Church Slavonic, the language used in Kievan Rus'. Additionally, many of the literary traditions of Russia and Ukraine can be traced back to Kievan Rus' literature, such as the epic poems that were popular in medieval Russia. One of the most famous examples of Kievan Rus' literature is the Primary Chronicle, a detailed account of the history of Kievan Rus' that was compiled in the 12th century. This chronicle is still studied by historians today, and is a testament to the enduring legacy of Kievan Rus'.

Kievan Rus' played a major role in the spread of Christianity throughout Eastern Europe. In the 10th century, Prince Vladimir the Great converted to Christianity and made it the official religion of Kievan Rus'. This conversion helped to cement Kievan Rus''s place as a major player in the Eastern European political and cultural scene, and helped to spread Christianity throughout the region.

The Byzantine Empire played a major role in this process, as it was a major center of Christian culture and learning at the time. Many of the priests and theologians who helped to spread Christianity throughout Kievan Rus' were trained in Byzantium, and brought back with them a deep knowledge of Christian doctrine and practice.

CHAPTER 3
THE COSSACK ERA (16ᵀᴴ-18ᵀᴴ CENTURIES)

———————— ❧ ————————

The Cossack era was a time of great importance in the history of Eastern Europe. This period was marked by the emergence of a unique culture and way of life that captivated the imaginations of people for centuries to come. From their legendary military prowess, to their traditional dances and music, the Cossacks were a fascinating people who left an indelible mark on the world. But what exactly was the Cossack era? And how did it shape the course of history?

This chapter will uncover the secrets of this remarkable period–from the rise of the first Cossack settlements in the 15th century to their involvement in major conflicts such as the Russo-Turkish War. The chapter will also explore the rich and complex history of the

Cossack era.

The Cossacks on horses

The Emergence and Development of Cossack Society

The origins of the Cossacks can be traced back to the 14th and 15th centuries, when Slavic and Turkic tribes began to settle in the region that is now Ukraine and southern Russia. These tribes were known for their fierce independence and warrior traditions, and they quickly became a powerful presence in the region. Over time, these tribes began to coalesce into larger groups, which eventually became the Cossack communities that we know today.

The word "Cossack" comes from the Turkic word "qazaq", which means "free man" or "adventurer". The Cossacks were known for their fierce loyalty to their communities and their willingness to fight for their independence. They were also known for their unique military tactics, which included riding horses and firing guns at the same time, as well as their distinctive clothing and customs.

Despite their reputation as fierce warriors, the Cossacks were also skilled traders and craftsmen. They were known for their fine embroidery, jewelry-making, and metalworking skills, as well as their ability to navigate the complex trade routes that crisscrossed the region. As the Cossack communities grew and flourished, they became a force to be reckoned with in Eastern Europe.

The Role of Cossacks in Defending Ukraine Against External Threats

The 16th and 17th centuries are often referred to as the "Golden Age" of the Cossacks. During this time, the Cossack communities grew in size and power, and they began to play an increasingly important role in the politics and culture of the region. The Cossacks were known for their fierce independence and their willingness to fight for their rights and freedoms.

One of the most famous Cossack leaders of the time was Bohdan Khmelnytsky, who led a rebellion against the Polish Lithuanian

Commonwealth in the mid-17th century. Khmelnytsky's rebellion was a turning point in Cossack history, and it helped to establish the Cossacks as a major political and military force in the region. Another famous Cossack leader was Stepan Razin, who led a rebellion against the Russian Empire in the late 17th century. Razin's rebellion was a significant challenge to the authority of the Russian tsars, and it helped to inspire other rebellions and uprisings throughout the region.

During the Golden Age, the Cossacks also developed a rich and distinctive culture that was based on their traditions and customs. They were known for their traditional dances and music, as well as their unique clothing and hairstyles. The Cossacks also developed their own language, which was a mixture of Ukrainian, Russian, and Turkic dialects. The Cossack era had a profound impact on the history of Ukraine and Russia. The Cossacks played an important role in the politics and culture of the region, and their traditions and customs continue to inspire artists and writers today.

One of the most important legacies of the Cossack era was the establishment of the Zaporozhian Sich, a semiautonomous Cossack state that existed in the region from the mid 16th to the late 18th century. The Sich was a center of Cossack culture and tradition, and it helped to establish the Cossacks as a major political and military force in the region. The Cossacks also played an important role in the politics of the region. They were involved in many of the major conflicts that shaped the course of Ukrainian and Russian history, including the Russo-Turkish War, the Napoleonic Wars, and the Crimean War.

The Cossacks were known for their unique military tactics and weaponry. They were skilled horsemen who were able to ride and shoot at the same time, and they developed unique tactics that were based on their horsemanship and their use of firearms. One of the most famous Cossack weapons was the "shashka", a curved sword that was used in close combat. The Cossacks were also known for their use of firearms, including pistols and muskets.

The Decline of the Cossack Era

The 18th and 19th centuries were a time of decline for the Cossacks. As the Russian Empire expanded into the region, the Cossacks found themselves increasingly marginalized and oppressed. Many Cossack communities were disbanded or destroyed, and their traditions and customs were suppressed.

Despite this, the Cossacks continued to play an important role in the history of the region. During the Russo-Turkish War of 1768-1774, the Cossacks played a key role in the Russian victory. They were also involved in the Napoleonic Wars and the Crimean War, where they fought bravely against some of the most powerful armies in Europe.

By the 20th century, the Cossacks had been largely assimilated into Russian and Ukrainian society. However, their traditions and customs continued to inspire artists, writers, and musicians throughout the region. Today, the Cossack culture is celebrated and commemorated in festivals and events throughout Ukraine and Russia.

The decline of the Cossack Era can be attributed to several key factors:

- Centralization of Power: As the Russian Empire expanded and consolidated its power, the Cossacks found themselves marginalized, and their autonomy gradually eroded.
- Changing Nature of Warfare: With the advent of modern military technology, the Cossacks' traditional style of warfare

became obsolete.

- Social and Economic Changes: As the region became more urbanized and industrialized, the traditional way of life of the Cossacks began to fade away.

The Impact of the Cossack Era on Ukrainian Culture, Art, and Literature

The Cossack culture is a rich and complex tradition that is based on centuries of history and tradition. The Cossacks were known for their fierce independence and their love of freedom, and this is reflected in their customs and traditions. One of the most distinctive aspects of Cossack culture is their traditional clothing. The Cossacks wore long, loose shirts and pants that were often decorated with intricate embroidery and patterns. They also wore tall boots and fur hats, which were both practical and stylish.

The Cossacks were also known for their love of music and dance. They developed a unique style of music that was based on traditional folk melodies and rhythms. Their dances were often fast and energetic, and they were performed with great enthusiasm and skill. Another important aspect of Cossack culture was their military traditions. The Cossacks were known for their fierce loyalty to their communities and their willingness to fight for their independence. They developed unique military tactics that were based on their horsemanship and their use of firearms.

The Cossack era produced a rich and diverse tradition of art and literature. Cossack artists were known for their fine embroidery, jewelry-making, and metalworking skills, as well as their ability to create intricate wood carvings and pottery. Cossack literature was also a vibrant and important tradition. Cossack writers and poets were known for their epic poems and ballads, which celebrated the heroic deeds of Cossack warriors and leaders.

Today, the Cossack era continues to be celebrated and commemorated in festivals and events throughout Ukraine and Russia. These events include traditional dances and music performances, as well as reenactments of famous battles and events from Cossack history. Many museums and cultural centers also focus on the history and traditions of the Cossacks. These institutions showcase Cossack art and artifacts, as well as providing educational materials and resources for people who are interested in learning more about this fascinating period of history.

CHAPTER 4
THE STRUGGLE FOR INDEPENDENCE (19TH-20TH CENTURIES)

The struggle for independence is a tale as old as time, and Ukraine has been no exception to this narrative. For centuries, Ukraine has been under the rule of various empires and regimes, each one stripping away their freedom and cultural identity. However, the people of Ukraine have never given up their fight for independence, and their story is one of resilience, perseverance, and hope. From the Cossack uprising of the 17th century to the recent Euromaidan protests of 2014, Ukraine's journey towards freedom has been long and arduous.

Third All-Ukrainian Military Congress, October 1917

The Political and Cultural Movements That Emerged in Ukraine

Ukrainian National Revival and the Struggle for Independence

Ukraine's relationship with Russia has been a complex and tumultuous one, dating back to the 18th century, when Ukraine became part of the Russian Empire. However, it wasn't until the 19th century that Ukrainian nationalism began to emerge as a force to be reckoned with. This movement was led by intellectuals and activists who sought to promote Ukraine's language, culture, and identity.

One of the most significant figures in this movement was Taras Shevchenko, a poet and artist who is considered to be the father of modern Ukrainian literature. Shevchenko's work celebrated Ukraine's history and culture, and he was an outspoken critic of the Russian Empire's policies towards Ukraine. His influence on Ukrainian nationalism cannot be overstated, and he is still revered by Ukrainians today.

Despite the efforts of Ukrainian nationalists, the Russian Empire continued to suppress Ukrainian language and culture. In 1863, the Tsarist government banned the Ukrainian language in schools, and Ukrainian publications were heavily censored. This repression only fueled the flames of Ukrainian nationalism, and by the turn of the 20th century, the movement had gained significant momentum.

The late 1980s and early 1990s saw a wave of revolutions across Eastern Europe, and Ukraine was no exception. In 1991, the Soviet Union collapsed, and Ukraine declared its independence. This was a momentous occasion for the Ukrainian people, who had fought for centuries to regain their freedom and cultural identity.

However, Ukraine's independence was not without its challenges. The country faced economic instability, political corruption, and a lack of infrastructure. Despite these obstacles, the Ukrainian people remained determined to build a better future for themselves and their country.

In 2004, Ukraine experienced another pivotal moment in its history with the Orange Revolution. This was a peaceful protest movement that saw Ukrainians take to the streets to protest against electoral fraud and corruption. The Orange Revolution was a turning point for Ukraine, as it marked the beginning of a new era of political and social activism.

The Orange Revolution also saw the emergence of pro-European sentiment in Ukraine. Many Ukrainians saw the European Union as a symbol of democracy and freedom, and they were eager to align themselves with Europe. This sentiment would come to a head in 2014 with the Euromaidan protests.

In 2014, Ukraine was once again plunged into crisis with the Euromaidan protests. These protests were sparked by the government's decision to abandon plans for closer ties with the European Union in favor of a closer relationship with Russia. The protests quickly grew in size and intensity, and they eventually led to the overthrow of the government.

The Euromaidan protests also coincided

with Russia's annexation of Crimea, a move that was met with widespread condemnation by the international community. The annexation of Crimea was a significant blow to Ukraine's sovereignty and territorial integrity, and it marked a new phase in Ukraine's fight for independence.

The Impact of World War I and the Russian Revolution on Ukraine

World War I was one of the most significant events in modern history, with its impact felt far beyond the battlefield. One of the nations that felt the brunt of the war was Ukraine, which was then a part of the Russian Empire. Ukraine had long been seeking greater autonomy, but the war brought with it a new set of challenges.

The war led to immense suffering for the Ukrainian people, with many forced to flee their homes and seek refuge elsewhere. The war also had a significant impact on the country's economy, with many businesses and farms destroyed in the fighting. The result was a significant loss of life, property, and resources, which had a lasting impact on the nation.

Despite the challenges, the war also led to the emergence of new political forces in Ukraine, with many people beginning to push for greater autonomy and even independence.

The seeds of revolution were sown, and the events that followed would change the course of Ukrainian history forever.

In 1917, the Russian Revolution brought about the collapse of the Tsarist regime and the emergence of the Soviet Union. Ukraine, which had been under the control of the Russian Empire, declared its independence and established the Ukrainian People's Republic. However, this new state was short-lived, as the Bolsheviks, under the leadership of Vladimir Lenin, quickly moved to take control of Ukraine.

The Bolshevik takeover sparked a bloody civil war that lasted for several years. During this time, Ukraine was devastated by violence, famine, and disease. The Bolsheviks were ruthless in their suppression of Ukrainian nationalism, and thousands of Ukrainians were executed or imprisoned for their political beliefs.

Despite the challenges, Ukraine continued to push for greater autonomy and independence. In 1918, the Ukrainian People's Republic declared independence, but its existence was short-lived. The Bolsheviks launched a series of offensives against the young nation, and by 1921, they had succeeded in bringing Ukraine under their control.

The Sovietization of Ukraine was a traumatic period in the nation's history, with many people forced to flee their homes or face persecution. The Soviet government sought to eliminate any challenges to its authority, and the result was a period of repression and violence. Despite the Bolsheviks' efforts to crush Ukrainian nationalism, the movement continued to grow. In 1922, Ukraine became a founding member of the Soviet Union, but the seeds of independence had already been planted.

The outbreak of World War II brought with it a new set of challenges for Ukraine. The country was once again caught in the middle of a conflict, and the fighting led to significant loss of life and property. The war also saw the emergence of new political forces in Ukraine, including nationalist groups that sought to challenge Soviet rule. The Ukrainian Insurgent Army (UPA) was one such group, which sought to establish an independent Ukrainian state.

The UPA was engaged in a prolonged struggle with Soviet forces, and the result was a period of violence and instability. Despite the challenges, the UPA remained committed to its goal of establishing an independent Ukraine, and the group continued to fight for its cause for many years.

The fall of the Soviet Union in 1991 was a momentous event in world history, and its impact on Ukraine cannot be overstated. The collapse of the Soviet Union led to the establishment of an independent Ukraine, which was recognized by the international community.

The establishment of an independent Ukraine was a significant milestone in the nation's history, and it marked the end of a long struggle for self-determination. The new nation faced many challenges, including economic difficulties and political instability, but it remained committed to its goal of becoming a prosperous and democratic country.

World War II and the Nazi Occupation of Ukraine

World War II had a profound impact on Ukraine, which was caught in the crossfire between Nazi and Soviet forces. The war began with the Nazi invasion of Poland in 1939, which was followed by the Soviet invasion of eastern Poland and the annexation of the Baltic states.

In 1941, Nazi forces invaded the Soviet Union, quickly overrunning much of Ukraine. The Nazis implemented a brutal occupation, killing millions of Ukrainian Jews and other minorities. Ukrainian nationalists also collaborated with the Nazis, hoping to achieve independence from the Soviet Union. The Soviet army eventually pushed the Nazis back, liberating Ukraine in 1944. However, the war had devastated the country, leaving behind a legacy of destruction and trauma that would last for decades.

After World War II, Ukraine became a key player in the Soviet Union's political and economic system. The country underwent rapid industrialization, with factories and collective farms springing up across the country. The Soviet government also established a system of education and healthcare, which helped to improve the standard of living for many Ukrainians.

However, the Soviet government was also known for its brutal repression of dissenting voices. Political opponents were arrested and executed, and censorship was rampant. The government also implemented policies that had devastating effects on the Ukrainian people, including the forced collectivization of agriculture and the Holodomor. Despite these hardships, many Ukrainians remained loyal to the Soviet system, seeing it as a way to achieve a better life for themselves and their families. This loyalty would be put to the test in the 1980s and

1990s, when the Soviet Union began to crumble.

The 1980s and 1990s were a time of great change in Ukraine and the Soviet Union as a whole. Economic stagnation, political corruption, and nationalist movements all contributed to growing unrest across the country. In 1991, the Soviet Union finally collapsed, marking the end of an era. Ukraine declared independence and began the long process of building a new nation. This was not without its challenges, however. The country faced economic and political turmoil, as well as ongoing tensions with Russia.

Despite these challenges, Ukraine has managed to establish itself as an independent nation with a unique culture and identity that's distinct from that of Russia. The country has also become an important player on the global stage, with a thriving economy and a vibrant cultural scene.

Despite its independence, Ukraine remains deeply connected to Russia, both culturally and economically. The two countries share a common history and language, and many Ukrainians have family and business ties in Russia. However, the relationship between the two countries has been strained in recent years, particularly since the 2014 Ukrainian revolution, which ousted pro-Russian President Viktor Yanukovych. Russia's annexation of Crimea and support for separatist rebels in Ukraine's eastern Donbas region have further inflamed tensions. Despite these challenges, Ukraine remains committed to its independence and its ties to the West.

From Language to Tradition: The Devastating Effects of Cultural Suppression in Ukraine

For centuries, Ukraine has been a land of diverse cultures and traditions, with a rich heritage that is deeply rooted in its language and customs. However, over the years, this cultural identity has been threatened by external forces that seek to suppress and erase it. The devastating effects of cultural suppression in Ukraine are widespread and far-reaching, impacting not only the language and traditions of its people but also their sense of identity and belonging. From the banning of Ukrainian language under Soviet rule to the recent conflicts in Eastern Ukraine, cultural suppression has resulted in a loss of historical knowledge, a decline in traditional practices, and a sense of disconnection from one's own cultural roots. In this article, we will explore the impact of cultural suppression in Ukraine, its historical context, and the efforts being made to preserve and revitalize Ukrainian language and traditions.

The suppression of Ukrainian language and culture is not a recent phenomenon. It has been happening for centuries. During the 18th and 19th centuries, the Russian Empire imposed policies that aimed to Russify Ukraine. These policies included the banning of Ukrainian language in schools and the media, and the promotion of Russian culture and language. The aim was to create a unified Russian state by eliminating cultural differences.

This policy continued under Soviet rule. In 1933, Stalin's government imposed a famine in Ukraine, killing millions of people. Known as the Holodomor, this man-made famine was designed to break the spirit of Ukrainian nationalism and force the country to submit to Soviet rule. The Soviet government also banned the use of Ukrainian language and promoted Russian culture, making it the only language used in official documents and media.

The effects of Soviet policies were far-reaching. Many Ukrainian intellectuals were arrested or killed, and Ukrainian language and culture were suppressed. The result was a loss of identity and a decline in traditional practices. The suppression of Ukrainian language and culture continued until the collapse of the Soviet Union in 1991.

The effects of cultural suppression in Ukraine have been devastating. The suppression of Ukrainian culture and language has led to a decline in traditional practices and a loss of historical knowledge. Many young people in Ukraine today do not speak Ukrainian fluently and have little knowledge of their cultural heritage. This has led to a sense of disconnection from one's own cultural roots and a loss of identity.

The suppression of Ukrainian culture has also led to a decline in traditional practices such as folk music, dance, and art. These practices were once an important part of Ukrainian culture, but they are now in danger of being lost forever. The suppression of Ukrainian language has also had an impact on literature. Many Ukrainian writers were forced to write in Russian, and Ukrainian literature was suppressed. As a result, Ukrainian literature has not received the recognition it deserves.

The Soviet Union's policies towards Ukraine were designed to suppress Ukrainian culture and promote Russian culture. The Soviet government banned the use of Ukrainian language in official documents and media, and promoted Russian culture as the only acceptable culture. This policy had a profound impact on Ukrainian culture, leading to a decline in traditional practices and a loss of historical knowledge.

The Soviet government also arrested and killed many Ukrainian intellectuals, including writers, artists, and musicians. This had a devastating impact on Ukrainian culture, as many of its most talented people were silenced. The suppression of Ukrainian culture continued until the collapse of the Soviet Union in 1991.

Since the collapse of the Soviet Union, there has been a resurgence of Ukrainian culture and language. Ukrainian language has been reintroduced in schools, and there have been efforts to promote Ukrainian culture. Folk music, dance, and art have become more popular, and there has been a renewed interest in Ukrainian literature.

The resurgence of Ukrainian culture has also led to a renewed sense of national pride. Many Ukrainians are proud of their cultural heritage and are working to preserve it. There are now many organizations in Ukraine dedicated to the preservation of Ukrainian culture and language.

Despite the resurgence of Ukrainian culture

and language, there are still many challenges. The conflict in Eastern Ukraine has had a profound impact on Ukrainian culture. Many Ukrainian-speaking areas have been occupied by Russian-backed separatists, and the Ukrainian language has been banned in these areas. The conflict has also led to a decline in traditional practices, as many people have been displaced from their homes and communities. This has made it difficult to pass on traditional practices to future generations.

The Ukrainian diaspora has played an important role in the preservation of Ukrainian culture. Ukrainians living abroad have been instrumental in promoting Ukrainian language and culture. They have established Ukrainian cultural centers and organized festivals and events to celebrate Ukrainian culture. The Ukrainian diaspora has also been active in supporting cultural preservation efforts in Ukraine. They have provided financial support for the preservation of historical sites and monuments, as well as for the production of Ukrainian literature, music, and art.

Cultural diversity is an important aspect of human society. It enriches our lives and helps us understand and appreciate different cultures. The suppression of culture is a loss not only for the people whose culture is being suppressed, but for all of humanity. Preserving cultural diversity is important for future generations. It ensures that traditional practices and knowledge are passed onto future generations. It also helps to maintain a sense of connection to one's own cultural roots.

The suppression of Ukrainian culture and language has had a devastating impact on the country. It has led to a decline in traditional practices and a loss of historical knowledge. However, there has been a resurgence of Ukrainian culture and language since the collapse of the Soviet Union. Ukrainians are proud of their cultural heritage and are working to preserve it. Despite the challenges, there is hope for the preservation of Ukrainian culture and language. The Ukrainian diaspora and organizations in Ukraine are working hard to promote Ukrainian culture and language. However, more needs to be done.

We must all take responsibility for preserving cultural diversity. We must support the efforts of those working to preserve Ukrainian culture and language. We must also educate ourselves and others about the importance of cultural diversity and the devastating effects of cultural suppression. Only by working together can we ensure that the rich cultural heritage of Ukraine is preserved for future generations.

CHAPTER 5
SOVIET UKRAINE (1917-1991)

U kraine boasts a rich and complex history that's deeply intertwined with that of the Soviet Union. From the early days of Soviet rule to the fall of the USSR, Ukraine played a crucial role in shaping the political, economic, and cultural landscape of the Soviet Union. Today, visitors to Ukraine can explore this fascinating history firsthand, discovering the remnants of Soviet architecture, the legacy of Soviet propaganda, and the stories of the people who lived through this tumultuous time. This chapter explores the history of Soviet Ukraine, from the early days of the Bolshevik revolution to the fall of the Berlin Wall.

The Establishment and Development of the Soviet Union in Ukraine

The early history of Ukraine is a story of migration and cultural exchange. The region's strategic location at the crossroads of Europe and Asia made it a hub for trade and commerce, and over the centuries, various groups and empires have vied for control of the territory. One of the earliest known groups to inhabit the region were the Scythians, a nomadic people who left behind rich burial sites and intricate gold jewelry. Later, the area was conquered by the Mongols, who ruled over it for centuries.

In the late 14th century, Ukraine came under the control of the Grand Duchy of Lithuania, which eventually merged with Poland to form the Polish-Lithuanian Commonwealth. This period saw the rise of the Cossacks, a group of fiercely independent warriors who played a crucial role in defending the region against foreign invaders. By the late 18th century, Ukraine had fallen under the control of the Russian Empire, which would ultimately shape its future as a Soviet republic. Despite centuries of foreign rule, however, Ukraine's unique culture and identity remained intact, setting the stage for the region's pivotal role in the Soviet era.

The Impact of the Soviet Policies on Ukrainian Society, Culture, and Politics

Joseph Stalin, the leader of the Soviet Union, had a particularly brutal impact on Ukraine. In the 1930s, he implemented a series of policies designed to crush Ukrainian nationalism and force the country to conform to Soviet ideology. One of the most devastating of these policies was the Holodomor, a man-made famine that was caused by the forced collectivization of agriculture. Stalin's government requisitioned grain from Ukrainian farmers, leaving many without enough food to survive. As a result, millions of Ukrainians died of starvation.

Stalin also implemented a policy of terror, systematically killing anyone who opposed the Soviet government. Ukrainian intellectuals, artists, and writers were particularly targeted, as Stalin saw them as a threat to Soviet control.

The result was a cultural void that lasted for decades, as many of Ukraine's best and brightest were silenced or killed. Despite these brutal policies, many Ukrainians remained loyal to the Soviet system, seeing it as a way to achieve a better life for themselves and their families. This loyalty would be put to the test during World War II, when Ukraine became a battleground for the Nazi and Soviet armies.

The impact of Stalin's policies in Ukraine left a dark legacy that still resonates today. The Soviet leader's brutal reign led to the deaths of millions, including countless Ukrainians who were subjected to forced collectivization, famine, and purges. These policies were aimed at suppressing Ukrainian culture and identity, and solidifying Soviet control over the region. The effects of these policies were devastating, leaving a lasting imprint on Ukraine's history and psyche. Despite the passage of time, the legacy of Stalin's policies continues to shape Ukraine's political and social landscape and serves as a reminder of the dangers of authoritarianism and the importance of safeguarding individual freedoms.

One of the key events that defined Stalin's reign in Ukraine was the Great Terror, a period of political repression and mass executions that targeted perceived enemies of the Soviet state. The purges were aimed at eliminating any perceived threats to Stalin's rule, including political opponents, intellectuals, and ethnic minorities.

In Ukraine, the Great Terror began in 1934 and continued until Stalin's death in 1953. During this time, thousands of Ukrainians were arrested, tortured, and executed without trial. The purges targeted not only political dissidents but also ordinary citizens, including farmers, teachers, and artists.

One of the most notorious events of the Great Terror was the "Night of the Murdered Poets" in August 1952, when thirteen prominent Ukrainian writers and intellectuals were executed by firing squad. The purge of the intelligentsia devastated Ukrainian culture and left a lasting impact on the country's intellectual and artistic traditions.

The Great Terror also had a lasting impact on Ukrainian society, creating an atmosphere of fear and suspicion that persisted long after Stalin's death. Many Ukrainians lived in constant fear of being denounced by their neighbors or colleagues and being arrested by the secret police. The legacy of the Great Terror continues to shape Ukraine's political and social landscape today.

Another key aspect of Stalin's policies in Ukraine was the use of forced labor camps, known as gulags, to suppress dissent and extract resources from the region. The gulags were used to imprison political dissidents, as well as ordinary citizens who were deemed to be enemies of the state.

In Ukraine, the gulags were used to extract resources from the region, including coal, timber, and other natural resources. Prisoners were forced to work long hours in harsh conditions, often without adequate food or medical care. Many died from disease, malnutrition, and exhaustion.

One of the most notorious gulags in Ukraine was the Karlag camp, located in the Karaganda region of Kazakhstan. The camp housed thousands of Ukrainian prisoners, who were forced to work in coal mines and other industries. The conditions in the camp were brutal, and many prisoners died from disease, starvation, and abuse.

The use of forced labor camps had a lasting impact on Ukrainian society, creating a culture of fear and mistrust that persisted long after Stalin's death. The legacy of the gulags continues to shape Ukraine's political and social landscape today.

Stalin's policies had a profound impact on Ukrainian society, transforming the country's culture, economy, and political system. One of the most significant effects of Stalin's policies was the forced collectivization of agriculture, which led to a famine that killed millions of Ukrainians.

The famine, known as the Holodomor, was a man-made disaster that was caused by Stalin's policies of forced collectivization and grain requisitioning. The policy led to a shortage of food in the countryside, and millions of Ukrainians died from starvation and disease.

The impact of the famine on Ukrainian society was devastating, and it had a lasting impact on the country's culture and identity. The famine was not officially recognized by the Soviet government until the 1990s, and it remains a deeply emotional and controversial topic in modern-day Ukraine.

Stalin's policies also had a lasting impact on Ukraine's political system, creating a centralized and authoritarian government that suppressed individual freedoms and dissent. The legacy of Stalin's policies continues to shape Ukraine's political and social landscape today, as the country struggles to build a democratic and free society. The impact of Stalin's policies can be seen in the country's politics, culture, and economy, as well as in the psyche of its people.

One of the most significant legacies of Stalin's policies is the ongoing conflict in eastern Ukraine, which has pitted pro-Russian separatists against the Ukrainian government. The conflict has its roots in Stalin's policies of forced migration and Russification, which created a large Russian-speaking population in the region.

The legacy of Stalin's policies can also be seen in Ukraine's political system, which continues to struggle with corruption and authoritarianism. The country's efforts to build a democratic and free society have been hampered by the legacy of Stalin's policies, which created a culture of fear and mistrust that is difficult to overcome.

Despite these challenges, Ukraine has made significant progress in recent years, with a new generation of leaders emerging who are committed to building a democratic and free society. The legacy of Stalin's policies continues to shape Ukraine's future, but the country is determined to move forward and build a better future for its people.

Holodomor - The Great Famine in Ukraine

Part of Stalin's dark legacy is the Holodomor. It was one of the most tragic and devastating events in Ukrainian history. It was a man-made famine that occurred in the early 1930s, caused by the forced collectivization of agriculture under Stalin's regime. The Soviet government requisitioned grain from Ukrainian farmers, leaving many without enough food to survive. As a result, millions of Ukrainians died of starvation. The exact number of victims is still a matter of debate, but estimates range from three to ten million people.

The Holodomor had a profound impact on Ukrainian society, leaving scars that would last for generations. It also highlighted the brutal nature of Stalin's regime and its willingness to sacrifice the lives of millions of people for the sake of ideological purity. Today, the Holodomor is widely recognized as an act of genocide. Ukrainian officials and activists have worked to raise awareness of the famine and to ensure that its victims are not forgotten.

The Ukrainian Resistance to Soviet Rule

The Ukrainian people have a rich history of resistance against foreign rule. Throughout its history, Ukraine has been invaded and occupied by various foreign powers, including the Mongols, Poles, Turks, and Russians. However, it was during the Soviet era that Ukrainian resistance reached its peak.

The Soviet Union was founded in 1922 and included Ukraine as one of its constituent republics. However, the Soviet regime was oppressive and totalitarian, and it sought to suppress any form of dissent. The Soviet Union was responsible for the deaths of millions of Ukrainians during the Holodomor famine of 1932-1933, and it continued to suppress Ukrainian culture and language throughout its rule.

Soviet rule in Ukraine began in 1919, after the Red Army defeated the Ukrainian National Republic. The Soviet regime was marked by political repression, forced collectivization, and mass deportations. The Soviet Union sought to impose its ideology on the Ukrainian people and to suppress any form of Ukrainian nationalism.

During the 1920s and 1930s, the Soviet regime launched a campaign to eliminate the kulaks, or prosperous peasants, who were seen as a threat to collectivization. This campaign led to the deaths of millions of Ukrainians during the Holodomor famine of 1932-1933. The Soviet regime continued to suppress Ukrainian culture and language throughout its rule, and it sought to impose Russian culture and language on the Ukrainian people.

Despite the Soviet regime's efforts to suppress Ukrainian nationalism, Ukrainian resistance emerged in the 1940s. The Ukrainian Insurgent Army (UPA) was founded in 1942, and sought to establish an independent Ukrainian state. The UPA was led by Stepan Bandera and Roman Shukhevych, who were both members of the Organization of Ukrainian Nationalists.

The UPA carried out a guerrilla war against the Soviet regime and its collaborators. The UPA was initially supported by the German occupation forces, but it later turned against the Germans and fought against both the Germans and the Soviets. The UPA's tactics included ambushes, sabotage, and assassinations of Soviet officials and collaborators.

The Ukrainian resistance was led by several key figures, including Stepan Bandera, Roman Shukhevych, and Taras Bulba-Borovets. Bandera was a prominent nationalist leader who sought to establish an independent Ukrainian state. Shukhevych was a military commander who led the UPA's military campaign against the Soviet regime. Borovets was a guerrilla fighter who was known for his daring raids against Soviet targets. These leaders were instrumental in organizing and leading the Ukrainian resistance against the Soviet regime. They inspired and motivated thousands of Ukrainians to join the resistance and fight for their independence.

The Ukrainian resistance used a variety of tactics and strategies in its fight against the Soviet regime. These included ambushes, sabotage, assassinations, and propaganda. The UPA also established a network of underground cells that provided logistical support and intelligence to the resistance fighters.

The UPA's tactics were effective in disrupting Soviet operations and weakening its control over Ukraine. The resistance fighters were able to carry out attacks on Soviet officials and collaborators, which made it difficult for the Soviet regime to maintain control over the population. The Ukrainian resistance had a significant impact on Soviet rule in Ukraine. The resistance weakened the Soviet regime's control over the population and disrupted its operations. The UPA's tactics also inspired other resistance movements throughout the Soviet Union. The Ukrainian resistance also had a cultural impact on Ukraine. It helped to promote Ukrainian culture and language and to inspire a sense of national pride among Ukrainians. The resistance fighters became heroes and symbols of Ukrainian resistance against foreign rule.

The Soviet regime responded to the Ukrainian resistance with brutal force. The Soviet security forces carried out mass executions, deportations, and forced resettlements of the Ukrainian population. The Soviet regime also launched a propaganda campaign to discredit the Ukrainian resistance and portray them as terrorists and criminals. The Soviet response to the Ukrainian resistance was marked by brutality and repression. The Soviet regime sought to crush any form of dissent and to maintain its control over Ukraine at all costs.

The Ukrainian resistance has also been the subject of criticism and controversy. Some have criticized the UPA for its collusion with the German occupation forces during World War II. Others have accused the UPA of carrying out atrocities against civilians and ethnic Poles.

These criticisms and controversies have been the subject of much debate and discussion in Ukraine. Some argue that the UPA was a legitimate resistance movement that fought against foreign occupation and oppression. Others argue that the UPA was a terrorist organization that carried out atrocities against civilians.

The legacy of Ukrainian resistance is still felt in modern-day Ukraine. The resistance fighters are celebrated as heroes and symbols of Ukrainian independence. The Ukrainian government has established monuments and memorials to honor the resistance fighters and to commemorate their struggle for independence. The Ukrainian language and culture have also been promoted in modern-day Ukraine. The Ukrainian government has implemented policies to protect and promote the Ukrainian language and to celebrate Ukrainian culture. This has helped to strengthen Ukraine's national identity and to promote a sense of national pride among Ukrainians.

CHAPTER 6
THE INDEPENDENT UKRAINE

The conflict between Russia and Ukraine has been ongoing since 2014. It has resulted in thousands of deaths, displacement of people, and political turmoil. The conflict is complex and multifaceted, with several root causes that have contributed to its escalation. This chapter will delve into the historical, political, and economic factors that have led to the Russia-Ukraine war. It will also examine the events that led to the annexation of Crimea, the role of ethnic tensions, and the impact of international politics on the conflict.

The Challenges Facing Ukraine in the Post-Soviet Era (Political, Economic, and Social Issues)

The future of Ukraine's fight for freedom is uncertain, but one thing is clear: the Ukrainian people will not give up their struggle for independence. The challenges facing Ukraine are significant, but the Ukrainian people have shown time and time again that they are willing to fight for what they believe in. Ukraine's journey towards independence has been marked by centuries of struggle, but it is also a story of resilience, perseverance, and hope. The Ukrainian people have faced immense challenges, but they have never given up their fight for freedom. As Ukraine looks towards the future, it will be the strength and determination of its people that will shape its destiny.

Ukraine's fight for independence has not

gone unnoticed by the international community. Countries around the world have voiced their support for Ukraine's sovereignty and territorial integrity, and many have imposed sanctions on Russia in response to its actions in Ukraine.

The United States and the European Union have been particularly vocal in their support for Ukraine, providing financial aid and diplomatic support to the country. Ukraine's fight for independence has become a global issue, and it is a testament to the strength and resilience of the Ukrainian people that they have been able to mobilize such support.

Ukraine has been struggling with its economy since it gained independence from the Soviet Union in 1991. Despite its potential, the country has been unable to transition to a modern, market-based economy, largely due to corruption, political instability, and external pressures from Russia.

After gaining independence from the Soviet Union in 1991, Ukraine inherited a centrally planned economy that was heavily dependent on Russia. The transition to a market-based economy was expected to be difficult, but initial optimism and potential were high. Unfortunately, the country was unprepared for the challenges that lay ahead. The privatization of state-owned enterprises was marred by corruption, and the sudden loss of subsidies from Russia left many sectors of the economy struggling to survive.

The country's economic struggles were compounded by political instability, including frequent changes in government and a lack of consensus on economic policy. In the absence of a clear vision for the future, Ukraine struggled to attract foreign investment, and the country's economy remained largely stagnant.

Ukraine's economy has been plagued by a number of challenges over the years. One of the most significant is corruption. According to Transparency International, Ukraine is one of the most corrupt countries in Europe, with a score of just 33 out of 100 on its Corruption Perceptions Index. Corruption is widespread at all levels of government, and has had a devastating impact on the country's economy. Another challenge facing Ukraine is its aging infrastructure. Many of the country's roads, bridges, and buildings are in a state of disrepair, which has made it difficult for businesses to operate and for goods to be transported. The country's energy sector is also in need of modernization, with many power plants and pipelines in urgent need of repair. Finally, Ukraine's labor market is highly inefficient. The country's rigid labor laws make it difficult for businesses to hire and fire workers, and the lack of a skilled workforce has made it difficult for businesses to compete in the global economy.

Corruption has had a devastating impact on Ukraine's economy. It has deterred foreign investment, discouraged domestic entrepreneurs, and led to a brain drain of talented professionals leaving the country. According to a report by the International Monetary Fund (IMF), corruption has cost Ukraine up to 2% of its GDP each year since 2015. Corruption has also had a negative impact on the country's public finances. According to the IMF, corruption has led to a loss of tax revenue, increased public spending, and a misallocation of public resources. This has made it more difficult for the government to invest in infrastructure, education, and healthcare, which are all essential for economic growth.

Ukraine's relationship with Russia has been a major factor in the country's economic struggles. Russia has used its energy exports to exert pressure on Ukraine, and has cut off gas supplies to the country on several occasions.

This has had a devastating impact on Ukraine's economy, as many industries rely on gas for heating and electricity. Russia has also annexed Crimea and supported separatist rebels in eastern Ukraine, which has led to a loss of territory and resources for Ukraine. The ongoing conflict has made it difficult for businesses to operate in the region, and has led to a loss of human capital as many people have been forced to flee their homes.

Despite the challenges facing Ukraine's economy, there have been some efforts to reform the country's economic system. The government has implemented a number of reforms aimed at reducing corruption, improving the business environment, and modernizing the country's infrastructure. One of the most significant reforms has been the establishment of an independent anti-corruption court.

The court has the power to investigate and prosecute cases of corruption, and has already secured a number of high-profile convictions. The government has also implemented a number of measures to improve the business environment, including simplifying the process of starting a business and reducing the regulatory burden on businesses. Finally, the government has launched a number of infrastructure projects aimed at modernizing the country's roads, bridges, and buildings. These projects have been funded in part by loans from international organizations such as the World Bank and the European Union.

Foreign aid has played a significant role in Ukraine's economic development. The country has received billions of dollars in loans and grants from international organizations and foreign governments. This aid has been used to support reforms, invest in infrastructure, and stabilize the country's finances. However, foreign aid alone is not enough to solve Ukraine's economic problems. The country must also address the root causes of its economic struggles, including corruption and political instability. Without these reforms, foreign aid will only provide a temporary solution to Ukraine's economic problems.

Despite the challenges facing Ukraine's economy, there are reasons to be optimistic about the country's future. The government has implemented a number of reforms aimed at reducing corruption and improving the business environment. Foreign aid has provided much-needed support for these reforms and for investment in infrastructure. However, much will depend on the country's ability to address the root causes of its economic struggles. Corruption and political instability remain major challenges, and it will take sustained effort and political will to overcome them. If Ukraine can address these challenges and continue to implement reforms aimed at modernizing the economy, there is reason to believe that the country's economy can thrive in the years ahead.

Ukraine's education and healthcare systems have struggled to provide adequate services to the population. The education system has been plagued by underfunding and outdated teaching methods, leading to a significant brain drain as many educated Ukrainians leave the country in search of better opportunities. The healthcare system has also struggled to provide adequate services, with many Ukrainians lacking access to basic healthcare services. The ongoing conflict in the Donbas region has further strained the healthcare system, with many hospitals and clinics damaged or destroyed.

Corruption has been a pervasive problem in Ukraine for many years, and it continues to be a significant challenge for the country today. In 2019, Ukraine ranked 126th out of 180 countries in the Corruption Perceptions Index, which measures public sector corruption. Corruption has undermined the rule of law, weakened democratic institutions, and impeded economic growth. Political instability has also been a significant challenge for Ukraine. Since gaining independence in 1991, Ukraine has had several changes in government, including the Orange Revolution in 2004 and the Euromaidan protests in 2014. These protests were sparked by allegations of election fraud and corruption, respectively. The protests led to the overthrow of the government in both cases, but the resulting governments have struggled to implement significant reforms.

A Timeline of the Major Events in the Political History of Ukraine Since It Became Independent from Russia in 1991

1991 – The leader of the Soviet Republic of Ukraine, Leonid Kravchuk, declared independence from Russia. In a presidential election and referendum, Ukrainians approved independence and elected Kravchuk as president.

1994 – Kravchuk loses to Leonid Kuchma in a free and fair presidential election.

1999 – In elections largely riddled with indiscretions, Kuchma is re-elected.

2004 – Victor Yanukovich, a pro-Russian candidate, is announced as president but protests that become known as the Orange Revolution are triggered by assertions of vote rigging. This forces a rerun of the elections. Viktor Yushchenko, a pro-Western former prime minister, is voted in as president.

2005 – Yushchenko becomes president and promises Ukrainians to lead the country out of the Kremlin's orbit, towards the EU and NATO. He assigns Yulia Tymoshenko, a former executive of an energy company as Prime Minister; however, after a bitter rivalry within the pro-Western camp, she is fired.

2008 – NATO makes a promise to Ukraine that one day it will join the coalition.

2010 – Tymoshenko loses to Yanukovich at the presidential elections. Ukraine and Russia agree to a gas pricing treaty in return for an extended lease for Russia's navy in Ukraine's Black Sea port.

2013 – In November, Yanukovich's administration suspended association negotiations and trade with the EU. They opt to re-establish economic ties with Russia, causing months-long mass protests in Kyiv.

2014 – The protests that take place mainly

around Kiev's Maidan square become violent and masses of protesters are slain.

February 2014 – The parliament decides to remove Yanukovich as president. He later flees. In a matter of days, parliament in Crimea, a region in Ukraine, is seized by armed men who also raise Russia's flag. After the March 16 referendum, Moscow extended the territory, which demonstrates overpowering support in Crimea for being a member of the Russian Federation.

April 2014 – The declaration of independence by Pro-Russian separatists in the Donbass region of eastern Ukraine led to the outbreak of fights, which has persisted intermittently until 2022, despite numerous attempts at ceasefires.

May 2014 – Petro Poroshenko, who is a politician and businessperson, became president with an agenda of the pro-Western camp.

July 2014 – A missile brought down MH17, a passenger plane flying from Amsterdam to Kuala Lumpur. All 298 passengers who were on board the plane were killed. Investigators linked the weaponry that was utilized to Russia. Russia denied its involvement.

2017 – An association treaty between the EU

and Ukraine opened the free trading of services and goods on the markets, and visa-free traveling for Ukrainians to the EU.

2019 – In Ukraine, a newly established Orthodox Church was officially acknowledged, causing frustration for the Kremlin. In April's presidential election, former actor and comedian Volodymyr Zelenskiy won against Poroshenko by vowing to combat corruption and end the conflict in eastern Ukraine. In July, Zelenskiy's political party, 'Servant of the People', won in the parliamentary election. During the same month, U.S. President Donald Trump requested Zelenskiy to investigate Joe Biden, his competitor in the U.S. presidential race, and Biden's son, Hunter, for possible business connections in Ukraine. The call ultimately led to an unsuccessful attempt to impeach Donald Trump.

March 2020 – In order to curb COVID-19, Ukraine went into its first lockdown.

June 2020 – The IMF approved a $5 billion financial rescue to assist Ukraine to survive a recession that was induced by COVID-19.

January 2021 – Zelenskiy appealed to U.S. president, Joe Biden, to allow Ukraine to become a member of NATO (North Atlantic

Treaty Organization).

February 2021 – Zelenskiy's administration enforced sanctions on Kremlin's very important associate in Ukraine and leader of the opposition, Viktor Medvedchuk.

Spring 2021 – Russia places a huge number of armed forces near the borders of Ukraine and says it's just a drill.

October 2021 – Ukraine angered Russia by using, for the first time in Eastern Ukraine, a Turkish Bayraktar TB2 drone.

Autumn 2021 – Russia started placing armed forces again near Ukraine's borders

December 7, 2021 – Biden warned Russia that they would extend Western economic sanctions if they invade Ukraine.

December 17 – Russia presented thorough security demands that included a lawfully binding agreement that NATO would give up any military action in Ukraine and in the East of Europe.

January 14 – Ukraine's government websites were hit by a cyber-attack warning them to "be afraid and expect the worst".

January 17 – Russian militaries started arriving

in the North of Ukraine (Belarus), for joint military exercises.

January 24 – NATO placed militaries as backup and reinforced Eastern Europe with more fighter jets and ships.

January 26 – Washington responded in writing to Russia about the security demand that they made–they repeated a pledge to the NATO's "open-door" approach while presenting "pragmatic" deliberations of Moscow's apprehensions.

January 28 – Russia's President, Vladimir Putin, said his country's key security demands had not been given the necessary attention.

February 2 – The United States said it would send an extra 3,000 armed forces to Romania and Poland to assist in shielding NATO associates in Eastern Europe so that the invasion does not affect them.

February 4 – At the Beijing Winter Olympics, Putin won the support of China when he demanded that Ukraine not be permitted to become a member of NATO.

February 7 – Emmanuel Macron, French President, was hopeful that the crisis would be resolved diplomatically after he met in the

Kremlin with Putin. Macron then visited Kyiv and praised Zelenskiy and the people of Ukraine for the "sang-froid".

February 9 – The U.S. State Department urged Americans living in Ukraine to leave the country as soon as possible as Biden said "things could go crazy quickly". Other nations also urged their citizens to leave Ukraine immediately.

February 14 – Zelenskiy urged Ukrainians to sing in unison Ukraine's national anthem and fly the country's flag on Feb 16, a day that was announced by some Western media houses as the day that Russia could possibly invade Ukraine.

February 15 – Russia announced that some of its armed forces would be going back to their base after their military exercises close to Ukraine's borders. Russia mocked the West about their forewarnings about an imminent invasion. The parliament in Russia asked Putin to acknowledge two Russian-backed breakaway states in Eastern Ukraine as being independent states.

February 18 – Michael Carpenter, U.S. ambassador to the Organization for Security and Cooperation, said possibilities are Russia has placed between 169,000- 190,000 armed forces in and close to Ukraine.

February 19 – Russia's tactical nuclear militaries held military exercises supervised by Putin.

February 21 – Macron said Putin and Biden principally agreed to hold talks over Ukraine. In an address on television, Putin said Ukraine is a vital part of Russia's history, the nation has never had a stable government, foreign powers are at the country's forefront, and it has a puppet government. Putin signed agreements to acknowledge sovereign states in the East of Ukraine as being independent and sent Russian militaries there.

February 22 – The UK, U.S., and their associates enacted sanctions on Russia's members of parliament, financial institutions, and other possessions. Germany halted the approval of the final accreditation of the Nord Stream 2 pipeline. In a television address, Putin made demands that Ukraine withdraw its armed forces and said the Minsk peace deal over autonomous states was no longer in place. He blamed Kyiv for ending the deal.

February 23 – Separatist leaders who were backed by Russia asked Russia to assist them in preventing violence from the Ukrainian military.

February 24 – Russia's head of State, Vladimir Putin authorized "special military operations" in the East of Ukraine, and in a televised address, he asked Ukrainian militaries to put down their weaponries. Russian militaries began artillery and missile attacks on Ukraine's air bases and forces, which struck regions in big cities.

The Events of the 2014 Ukrainian Revolution and Their Impact On Ukrainian Politics and Society

The history of the Russia-Ukraine conflict can be traced back to the Soviet era when Ukraine was part of the Soviet Union. After the collapse of the Soviet Union in 1991, Ukraine became an independent state. However, Russia continued to view Ukraine as part of its sphere of influence. In 2014, the pro-Russian Ukrainian President, Viktor Yanukovych, was ousted in a popular uprising. The Ukrainian government that replaced Yanukovych was pro-Western and sought closer ties with the European Union. Russia saw this as a threat to its interests and responded by annexing Crimea, a region in Ukraine that has a significant ethnic Russian population.

The key players in the Russia-Ukraine

conflict are Russia, Ukraine, the European Union, and the United States. Russia has been accused of providing military support to separatist rebels in Ukraine's eastern regions. Ukraine has accused Russia of annexing Crimea and supporting separatist rebels. The European Union and the United States have imposed economic sanctions on Russia in response to its actions in Ukraine. The conflict has also attracted the involvement of other countries, including Turkey, which has supported Ukraine, and Belarus, which has remained neutral.

Causes of the Conflict
Political and Economic Factors - The Russia-Ukraine conflict has several political and economic root causes. One of the main political causes is Ukraine's desire to move closer to the European Union and NATO. Russia sees this as a threat to its interests and has responded with aggression. Another political factor is the Ukrainian government's corruption and lack of accountability, which has led to discontent among the population. Economic factors have also played a role in the conflict. Ukraine's economy has been struggling, and it has been heavily dependent on Russia for gas supplies. Russia has used this dependence as a tool to exert influence over Ukraine.

Cultural and Ethnic Factors - Cultural and ethnic factors have also contributed to the Russia-Ukraine conflict. Ukraine has a significant ethnic Russian population, particularly in Crimea and the eastern regions. The annexation of Crimea was partly motivated by Russia's desire to protect the ethnic Russians living there. The Ukrainian government's attempts to promote Ukrainian language and culture have also been viewed as a threat by the ethnic Russian population.

Geopolitical and Strategic Factors - Geopolitical and strategic factors have played a role in the Russia-Ukraine conflict. Ukraine is strategically located between Russia and Europe, and it has been a battleground for influence between the two. Russia sees Ukraine as a buffer zone between itself and NATO. The annexation of Crimea has given Russia a strategic foothold in the Black Sea, which is of significant military importance. The conflict has also been influenced by the United States' desire to promote democracy and human rights in the region.

International Response to the Conflict

The international community has responded to the Russia-Ukraine conflict with a mix of sanctions, diplomacy, and military support. The

European Union and the United States have imposed economic sanctions on Russia, which have had a significant impact on its economy. Diplomatic efforts have been made to find a peaceful solution to the conflict, but they have been largely unsuccessful. The United States has provided military aid to Ukraine, including weapons and training. The conflict has also attracted the attention of the United Nations, which has called for a peaceful resolution to the conflict. The conflict has also resulted in a humanitarian crisis, with thousands of people displaced and many casualties. The conflict has had a significant impact on civilians, particularly those living in the conflict zones. There have been reports of human rights abuses, including torture and extrajudicial killings. The conflict has also had a significant impact on the economy, infrastructure of the affected regions, and the leadership of the country.

The Pre-Zelensky Era

The pre-Zelensky era was marked by the presidency of Viktor Yanukovych, who came to power in 2010. Yanukovych was a controversial figure, known for his pro-Russian stance and alleged ties to organized crime. His presidency was marked by widespread corruption, political repression, and the erosion of democratic institutions. In 2013, Yanukovych's decision to abandon a planned association agreement with the European Union sparked massive protests, known as the Euromaidan revolution. The protests, which lasted for several months, were fueled by popular anger at Yanukovych's corruption and authoritarianism, as well as a desire for closer ties with Europe. The revolution ultimately led to Yanukovych's ouster in February 2014. However, Yanukovych's removal from power did not bring an end to Ukraine's political crisis. The country was soon plunged into a conflict with Russian-backed separatists in the eastern Donbass region, leading to a protracted war that has claimed over 13,000 lives to date.

Following Yanukovych's ouster, Ukraine held presidential elections in May 2014, which were won by Petro Poroshenko. Poroshenko, a wealthy businessman with experience in government and politics, inherited a country in crisis. His presidency was marked by ongoing conflict in the Donbass region, as well as economic challenges and political tensions. Under Poroshenko's leadership, Ukraine pursued a pro-Western foreign policy, seeking closer ties with Europe and the United States. However, the country's relations with Russia remained strained, with Moscow annexing

Crimea in March 2014 and providing support to separatists in eastern Ukraine.

Poroshenko's presidency was also marked by efforts to combat corruption and reform Ukraine's political and economic systems. However, progress on these fronts was limited, and Ukraine's oligarchs continued to wield significant influence over the country's politics; that is how Ukraine's political landscape became characterized by a diverse array of political parties and factions that reflect the country's complex history and societal divisions. Some of the most prominent political parties in Ukraine include:

- The Servant of the People Party, which was founded in 2018 by comedian and actor Volodymyr Zelensky. The party is currently in power, with Zelensky serving as president.
- The Opposition Platform - For Life, which is aligned with Russia and seeks closer ties with Moscow.
- The European Solidarity Party, which was founded by Poroshenko and advocates for closer ties with Europe and the West.
- The Batkivshchyna Party, which is led by former prime minister Yulia

Tymoshenko and advocates for economic and social reforms.

In addition to these parties, there are numerous factions and independent politicians who hold significant sway over Ukraine's politics. The country's political scene is characterized by shifting alliances and coalitions, as well as a lack of clear ideological divides. Ukraine's oligarchs, a group of wealthy businessmen who amassed power and influence following the collapse of the Soviet Union, have been a major force in the country's politics and economy. The oligarchs control large swaths of the country's media, energy, and industrial sectors, and often use their wealth to influence political outcomes. The influence of the oligarchs has been a major obstacle to democratic reform and good governance in Ukraine. Many of the country's political and economic systems are designed to benefit the interests of the oligarchs, rather than the broader public. Efforts to combat oligarchic influence and corruption have been a key focus of Ukraine's political reform efforts in recent years. However, progress on these fronts has been limited, and the oligarchs continue to exert significant influence over Ukraine's politics and economy.

Corruption has long been a major issue in Ukraine, with many politicians and officials using their positions for personal gain. The country ranks poorly on international measures of corruption, and efforts to combat corruption have been a key focus of Ukraine's political reform efforts. Under Poroshenko's presidency, there were some efforts to combat corruption, including the establishment of a National Anti-Corruption Bureau and the adoption of anti-corruption legislation. However, progress on these fronts was limited, and corruption remains a major issue in Ukraine. The current Zelensky administration has also made anti-corruption efforts a priority, with the establishment of a new anti-corruption court and the dismissal of several officials accused of corruption. However, the success of these efforts remains to be seen.

Ukraine has a vibrant civil society and media landscape, with numerous NGOs, activist groups, and independent media outlets. These organizations have played an important role in promoting democratic reform, human rights, and transparency in Ukraine. However, civil society and media organizations in Ukraine face numerous challenges, including threats and intimidation from powerful interests, limited resources, and a lack of legal protections. Many journalists and activists have been subject to violence and harassment in recent years, highlighting the dangers of their work.

Ukraine's geopolitical position has been a major driver of its politics and foreign policy. The country sits at the intersection of Europe and Russia, and has long been a pawn in the broader geopolitical struggles between these two powers. Under Yanukovych, Ukraine pursued a pro-Russian foreign policy, seeking closer ties with Moscow and distancing itself from the West. However, this policy was deeply unpopular among many Ukrainians, and ultimately led to Yanukovych's ouster Since then, Ukraine has pursued a pro-Western foreign policy, seeking closer ties with Europe and the United States. However, the country's relations with Russia remain fraught, with ongoing conflict in the Donbass region and Moscow's annexation of Crimea.

Ukraine's political landscape is marked by numerous challenges, including corruption, oligarchic influence, geopolitical tensions, and ongoing conflict in the Donbass region. These challenges have hindered democratic reform and good governance in Ukraine, and have contributed to a sense of disillusionment and frustration among many Ukrainians. Efforts to address these challenges have been ongoing, but progress has been slow and limited. However, the election of Zelensky in 2019 represented a potential turning point for Ukraine, with the promise of new leadership and fresh ideas.

The Impact of Volodymyr Zelensky's Presidency on Ukraine

Zelensky's presidency was a significant shift in Ukraine's political landscape, as he came to power with no prior political experience. Volodymyr Zelensky is a Ukrainian comedian, screenwriter, and producer who became famous for his satirical television series "Servant of the People", in which he played a high school teacher who became president of Ukraine after a viral video of his anti-corruption rant. In 2019, Zelensky decided to run for the presidency in real life, and to everyone's surprise, he won with 73% of the vote, defeating the incumbent Petro Poroshenko.

Since the election of Volodymyr Zelensky as the President of Ukraine, the country has been undergoing some significant political changes. His victory marked a significant shift in Ukrainian politics, with the traditional ruling elites being replaced by a new generation of leaders. Since taking office, Zelensky has initiated several reforms aimed at improving the country's economy, fighting corruption, and ending the conflict with Russia-backed separatists in eastern Ukraine. These changes have had a profound impact on Ukraine's political landscape, with some applauding Zelensky's efforts while others remain skeptical.

Zelensky's campaign was centered around anti-corruption, economic reforms, and ending the war in Eastern Ukraine. He promised to clean up Ukraine's political system and to create a level playing field for businesses. He also pledged to tackle the oligarchs who had dominated Ukraine's economy for decades. Zelensky's campaign was notable for its use of social media and modern communication tools, which helped to mobilize the younger electorate.

Since taking office, Zelensky's government has implemented several significant reforms. One of the most notable is the judicial reform, which aimed to reduce political influence over the courts and to improve the transparency and efficiency of the judiciary. Another major reform is the land reform, which seeks to create a market for agricultural land and to boost agricultural productivity. Zelensky's government has also introduced a new law on public procurement, which aims to increase transparency and reduce corruption in government procurement.

Zelensky's policies have had a significant impact on the country's economy. In 2019, Ukraine's GDP grew by 3.2%, which was the highest rate in seven years. The government has also taken steps to reduce the budget deficit, which has been a major issue for the country in recent years. However, Ukraine still faces significant economic challenges, including high levels of debt, a weak currency, and a large informal economy.

Zelensky's presidency has been a mixed bag in terms of public perception. While he remains popular among his supporters, there has been some disillusionment with his government's performance. Many of his campaign promises have yet to be fulfilled, and there are concerns that corruption remains a problem in Ukraine. However, Zelensky's government has been credited with improving the business climate in

Ukraine and boosting economic growth.

Zelensky's presidency has faced opposition from various groups, including the political opposition, civil society groups, and oligarchs. The political opposition has accused Zelensky of being a puppet of the oligarchs and of failing to deliver on his promises. Civil society groups have criticized Zelensky's government for its lack of progress on human rights issues, including the rights of minorities and the LGBT community. Oligarchs, who have been targeted by Zelensky's anti-corruption drive, have launched a media campaign against him.

Ukraine's relationship with Russia has been a major factor in the country's politics since its independence in 1991. The conflict with Russia-backed separatists in eastern Ukraine has been ongoing since 2014 and has had a significant impact on the country's politics and economy. Zelensky has promised to end the conflict and has taken steps to negotiate with Russia.

Zelensky sought to improve relations with Russia, which have been strained since the annexation of Crimea in 2014. Zelensky met with Russian President Vladimir Putin several times, and there were some small steps towards resolving the conflict in Eastern Ukraine. Zelensky also sought to deepen Ukraine's ties with the European Union and NATO, and there had been some positive developments on that front as well.

Zelensky's policies towards Russia have been controversial. Some have accused him of being too soft on Russia and not doing enough to defend Ukraine's sovereignty. Others have praised his efforts to negotiate a peaceful resolution to the conflict. The conflict in eastern Ukraine remains unresolved, and it is unclear what impact Zelensky's policies will have on the situation.

Zelensky's presidency has faced several challenges, both internal and external. One of the biggest challenges has been the ongoing conflict in Eastern Ukraine, which has claimed thousands of lives and displaced millions of people. Zelensky has made efforts to resolve the conflict, but progress has been slow. Another challenge has been the COVID-19 pandemic, which hit Ukraine hard and put a strain on the country's healthcare system. Zelensky's government also faced criticism for its handling of the pandemic.

One of the major challenges facing Zelensky's presidency has been the economic crisis affecting Ukraine since Russia's annexation of Crimea in 2014. Russia started imposing a trade embargo on Ukraine, which has had a significant impact on the country's economy. Inflation reached as high as 33% in 2018, and some 600,000 Ukrainians lost their jobs due to the economic problems. This posed a challenge to Zelensky because he promised that his presidency would be dedicated to turning Ukraine around economically by creating jobs and public investment opportunities for Ukrainians. With joblessness rates reaching 40%, and the Russian trade embargo still in effect, Zelensky failed to deliver on one of his promises.

The future prospects for Ukraine's political landscape under Zelensky's presidency are uncertain. While Zelensky has made progress on some fronts, there are still many challenges to be addressed. The conflict in Eastern Ukraine remains a major obstacle to peace and stability, and corruption remains a significant problem. Zelensky's government will need to continue to implement reforms and address these challenges if it wants to maintain public support and achieve its goals.

The War With Russia 2021 Onwards

As of 2021, the Russia-Ukraine conflict is ongoing, with no clear solution in sight. The conflict has entered a stalemate, with both sides dug in and unwilling to compromise. The annexation of Crimea remains a significant obstacle to peace. The conflict has also been complicated by the COVID-19 pandemic, which has made diplomatic efforts more difficult. The future prospects for the conflict remain uncertain, but a peaceful resolution will require compromise and a commitment to finding a lasting solution.

The impact of the Ukraine War was devastating. The war caused the displacement of over two million people, with many forced to flee their homes and seek refuge in other parts of Ukraine or abroad. The war also resulted in the loss of over 13,000 lives, including civilians and soldiers. The destruction of infrastructure, homes, and businesses was widespread, and the Ukrainian economy suffered a severe blow.

The war also had a psychological impact on the Ukrainian people. Many had to deal with the trauma of losing loved ones, homes, and livelihoods. The conflict also created a sense of insecurity and fear, with many living in constant fear of shelling and violence. The war also had a significant impact on the mental health of the population, with many suffering from anxiety, depression, and post-traumatic stress disorder.

Despite the devastation caused by the war, Ukraine has made significant efforts towards post-war recovery and reconstruction. The Ukrainian government has implemented a range of initiatives to support those affected by the war and rebuild the country. These initiatives include the reconstruction of infrastructure, including roads, bridges, and public buildings. This has been a priority for the Ukrainian government. The government has invested in rebuilding damaged infrastructure and constructing new buildings to replace those destroyed during the conflict. This effort has been supported by international aid, which has helped to fund reconstruction projects. The Ukrainian government has also provided support for those displaced by the war. The support has included financial assistance, housing, and other forms of aid. The government has also worked to facilitate the return of displaced persons to their homes and communities.

Another initiative has been the economic reconstruction, in which the government has implemented measures to support economic recovery, including investment in key sectors such as agriculture, energy, and infrastructure. The government has also implemented reforms to improve the business climate and attract foreign investment.

Despite the progress made in post-war recovery and reconstruction, Ukraine still faces significant challenges such as economic challenges of an economy that was ailing before the war and has become worse since the conflict began. The country faces high levels of debt, inflation, and unemployment. The conflict has also led to the loss of key economic sectors, such as manufacturing and mining. Another challenge that Ukraine faces is political instability in recent years, which has made it difficult to implement reforms and attract foreign investment. Corruption and political interference in the judiciary have also been significant challenges. The other challenge is the security risks. The conflict in the Donbass region is ongoing, and there is a risk of further escalation. The conflict has also led to the proliferation of weapons and the rise of criminal groups, which pose a threat to security.

Despite the challenges faced, Ukraine has made significant progress in its post-war recovery efforts. The country has implemented reforms in key sectors and attracted foreign investment. Infrastructure has been rebuilt, and support has been provided to displaced persons. The Ukrainian government has also made efforts to address corruption and improve the business climate.

Ukraine's post-war reconstruction efforts present significant opportunities for investment. The country has a skilled workforce, abundant natural resources, and a strategic location. The government has implemented reforms to improve the business climate, and foreign investment is welcome. Investment opportunities exist in a range of sectors, including agriculture, energy, infrastructure, and technology. The Ukrainian government has also implemented measures to support foreign investors, including tax incentives and streamlined procedures for obtaining permits and licenses.

Lessons Learnt from Ukraine's Post-War Recovery

Ukraine's post-war recovery efforts provide valuable lessons for other countries facing similar challenges. These lessons include the importance of political stability. Political stability is crucial for implementing reforms and attracting investment. Ukraine's political instability has been a significant challenge, and other countries can learn from this experience. Another lesson is about the role of international aid. International aid can play a crucial role in supporting post-war recovery efforts. The international community can provide financial and technical assistance to help rebuild infrastructure, support displaced persons, and promote economic recovery. And lastly, the most crucial lesson is the need for transparency and accountability. Transparency and accountability are essential for ensuring that aid is used effectively and that corruption is addressed. Ukraine's experience highlights the importance of transparency and accountability in post-war recovery efforts.

Ukraine's post-war recovery efforts have been impressive, given the scale of the devastation caused by the conflict. The country has shown resilience and determination in rebuilding its infrastructure, supporting displaced persons, and promoting economic recovery. International aid has played a crucial role in supporting these efforts. However, Ukraine still faces significant challenges, including economic difficulties, political instability, and security risks. The country must continue with reforms to address these challenges and attract foreign investment. The Ukrainian people have shown resilience and determination in the face of adversity, and their future prospects look bright.

CONCLUSION

In conclusion, Ukraine's history is complex and multifaceted, with a long and storied past that has been shaped by a series of significant events. From the chaos of war to the upheaval of revolution, Ukraine has faced many challenges over the years, but it has remained resilient and determined.

Today, Ukraine is a nation that is still grappling with its past, but it is also looking towards the future with optimism and hope. The country is home to many talented and dedicated people, who are working tirelessly to build a brighter future for themselves and their country. As we look back at Ukraine's history, we can see how events such as World War I and the Russian Revolution have played a significant role in shaping the nation. But we can also see how the people of Ukraine have remained committed to their goal of self-determination and independence, and how they have continued to struggle and persevere in the face of adversity.

As Ukraine moves forward, it will continue to face many challenges, but it will also have many opportunities to build a brighter and more prosperous future for itself and its people. And as we look ahead, we can be confident that Ukraine's rich and complex history will continue to shape the nation for many years to come.

The election of Zelensky represents a potential turning point for the country, with the promise of new leadership and fresh ideas. However, addressing the deep-seated challenges facing Ukraine's politics and governance will require sustained effort and commitment. The country's civil society and media organizations will continue to play a critical role in promoting transparency, accountability, and democratic reform. Ultimately, the fate of Ukraine's political landscape will be determined by the actions of its leaders and citizens. With continued dedication and perseverance, Ukraine can overcome its challenges and build a brighter future for all Ukrainians.

APPENDIX

The Timeline of Some of the Major Events From the Mid-800s to 1994 That Shaped Ukraine's Identity and Political Landscape

Mid 800s – The Scandinavians established a trade route along the Dnieper river

988 – Prince Volodymyr was baptized in Chersonesus

1037 – The completion of the Santa Sofia Cathedral

1240 – Mongol army under Batu Khan captured Kiev

1362 – Kiev was captured by the Lithuanian army under Grand Duke Algirdas

1363 – Lithuanian won over the Mongols at the Battle of Blue Waters

1386 – Grand Duke Iogaila of Lithuania was crowned as Poland's King after he married Queen Jadwiga of Poland

Early 1400s – The first Cossack outposts were established

1553 – The Zaporozhian Sich was established

1569 – Union of Lublin created the Polish–Lithuanian Commonwealth

1596 – Union of Brest created the Uniate church

1648 – Khmelnitsky Rebellion began

1654 – Pereiaslav Agreement led to the Russo-

Polish War. Khmelnitsky accepted protection from Russia

1657–1686 – A period known as 'The Ruin' that was characterized by civil unrest and the interference of foreign forces in Ukraine. The war for the control of Ukraine broke-out between the Cossacks, Turks, Poland, and Russia

1686 – 'Eternal Peace' between Poland and Russia handed over land that belonged to the Cossacks in the East of the Dnieper and Kiev to Russian rule

1687 – Ivan Mazepa was appointed as Hetman of Russian-ruled Ukraine

1708 – The Swedish army under Charles XII entered Ukraine. Mazepa declared support for Charles

1709 – The Battle of Poltava began and Peter the Great defeated the Swedes and Cossacks

1773 – Poland's first partition took place. Galicia turned into the crown land of the Austrian Empire

1774 – Treaty of Kuchuk Kainarji ended the Russo-Ottoman war

1775 – Catherine the Great destroyed the Zaporozhian Sich

1781 – Catherine dissolved the Hetmanate

1783 – Catherine annexed Crimea

1795 – Poland's third and final partition took

place

1830–1831 – November Insurrection – The unsuccessful overthrow of the Russian rule in Ukraine, Belorussia (Belarus), certain regions of Lithuania, Polish regions of Western Russia, as well as the Congress Kingdom of Poland

1840 – Tara Shevchenko published his book of poems titled 'Kobzar'

1847 – Shevchenko was arrested and exiled

1848 – The 'Spring of Nations' began. The Polish uprisings in Lviv and Cracow began. Ukraine's Supreme Ruthenian Council declared loyalty to the Hapsburgs

1861 – Municipal council was elected in Lviv and Vienna with limited representation of Ukrainians

1863–1864 – The January Uprising – An insurrection that took place in the Russian Kingdom of Poland with the aim at the restoring the Polish-Lithuanian

1876 – Edict of Ems banned all teaching and publishing in Ukrainian language in the Russian empire

1881 – Anarchists assassinated Alexander II. The occurrence of Anti-Jewish violence (Pogroms) in Yelizavetgrad (Kirovohrad), Odessa, and Kiev

1890 – The first Ukrainian political party, the Ruthenian-Ukrainian Radical Party was established in Lviv

1905 – Nicholas II made democratic concessions during mass protests and strikes. Anti-Jewish violence (Pogroms) in Nikolayev (Mykolayiv), Kherson, and Odessa

1908 – Myroslav Sichynskyi, who was a Ukrainian student and radical socialist, assassinated Count Andrzej Potocki, Polish governor of Galicia

March 1917 – The Russian Revolution collapsed the Romanov Empire and Nicholas II stepped down. Central Council of Ukraine formed in Kiev

October 1917 – The Bolshevik Revolution, the first prolific Marxist take-over in history took place in Petrograd (St. Petersburg)

January 1918 – The Red Army captured Kiev. The Ukrainian Rada fled after declaring Ukraine's independence

March 1918 – Russia recognized Ukraine`s independence by signing the Treaty of Brest-Litovsk. The German army occupied Kiev

November 1918 – West Ukrainian National Republic was declared in Lviv. Ukrainian government fled to Stanyslaviv (Ivano-Frankivsk) during the synchronized Polish uprising

December 1918-August 1921 – The war for the control of Ukraine between 'Cossack' peasant bands, and the White, Red, Polish and Ukrainian troops breaks out

1923 – The Polish sovereignty received formal recognition from its allies in Galicia. Korenizatsiya launched in Soviet Ukraine

1929 – Collectivisation and 'Dekulakization' began in Ukraine

1929-1933 – The deportation of up to twelve million 'kulaks'

1930 – Ukrainian purges begin. Polish 'pacification' campaign in Galicia

1932–1933 – Up to five million peasants died of hunger in Soviet Ukraine

1937–1939 – Second wave of purges swept the Soviet Union. Up to one million Soviets were executed and up to twelve million were sent to camps

1939 – The Soviet Union and Nazi Germany signed the Ribbentrop–Molotov. It gave way for the parties to jointly invade and occupy Poland. Soviet Union occupied Galicia

June 1941 – Germany invaded the Soviet Union. The deportation and massacre of Jews living in Ukraine happened

1942 – The Ukrainian Insurgent Army (UPA) was established

1943–1944 – Soviet army recaptured Ukraine

May 1944 – The Crimean Tatars were deported

1947 – The last UPA units were rounded up in

Poland. The Ukrainians living in Poland were deported to the Soviet Union and newly acquired land that belonged to Germany

1954 – Crimea was handed over by Khrushchev to the Ukrainian SSR

1965–1966 – The Ukrainian 'sixtiers' were arrested and put on a show trial

1972 – Volodymyr Shcherbytsky was appointed as First Secretary of the Ukrainian Communist Party. Ukrainian intelligentsia were arrested in huge numbers

1976 – The Ukrainian Helsinki Group was established

1986 – The Chernobyl Accident – A power plant in Ukraine exploded, killing two workers on the night of the explosion and a further 28 people a few weeks later from exposure to extreme radiation

1988 – The first anti-communist protests took place in Kiev and Lviv

1989 – Shcherbytsky was fired. Rukh held its founding senate. Uniate parishes received legal recognition

March 1990 – Ukraine's Supreme Soviet semi-democratic elections took place

September–October 1990 – A mass protest and student hunger strike broke out in Kiev

October 1990 – The Ukrainian Autocephalous Orthodox Church became legally recognized

August 1991 – Soviet coup d'état attempt – The Communist hard-liners tried to forcefully seize the country from Russia's Mikhail Gorbachev. Ukraine's Supreme Soviet declared independence

December 1991 – Leonid Kravchuk was elected as Ukraine's first president

January 1994 – Trilateral Statement between America, Russia, and Ukraine was signed. In the agreement, Ukraine agreed to surrender its nuclear weapons to Russia to be destroyed

July 1994 – Leonid Kuchma was elected as Ukraine's second president

Key Figures in Ukrainian History
Volodymyr the Great

Volodymyr the Great

The reign of Ukraine's most influential ruler, Volodymyr the Great was a pivotal moment in

Ukraine's history, and his conversion to Christianity changed the course of the country's development. Volodymyr the Great was born in 958 AD, the son of Sviatoslav I, the Grand Prince of Kiev. His early life was marked by political turmoil, as his father fought for control over the Kievan Rus', a federation of Eastern Slavic tribes that dominated the region. Volodymyr was one of Sviatoslav's many sons, and after his father's death, he had to compete with his brothers for control over Kiev.

Despite the challenges he faced in his early years, Volodymyr proved to be a skilled and ambitious leader. He consolidated his power by defeating his rivals, expanding the Kievan Rus', and establishing diplomatic ties with neighboring kingdoms. His reign was marked by impressive accomplishments, such as the construction of the Saint Sophia Cathedral in Kiev, the establishment of a system of justice, and the creation of a written legal code.

To understand the significance of Volodymyr's reign, it is important to consider the historical context of Ukraine during this period. The Kievan Rus' was a vast federation of tribes that had emerged in the 9th century, following the collapse of the Khazar Khaganate. The Kievan Rus' controlled vast territories that encompassed modern-day Russia, Ukraine, and Belarus, and it played a pivotal role in the development of Eastern Europe.

During the 10th century, the Kievan Rus' was a highly decentralized federation, with each tribe having its own ruler and customs. The region was also plagued by political instability, as different factions vied for control over the federation. It was in this context that Volodymyr emerged as a powerful leader, capable of consolidating power and expanding the federation's influence.

Volodymyr was born in a time of great political turmoil, as his father fought for control over the Kievan Rus'. His early years were marked by conflict and uncertainty, as he had to compete with his brothers for control over Kiev. In 980 AD, Volodymyr defeated his brother Yaropolk and established himself as the ruler of the Kievan Rus'.

Volodymyr was a skilled and ambitious leader, and he quickly set about consolidating his power. He established a system of justice, creating a written legal code that regulated the behavior of his subjects. The code was based on the principles of justice and fairness, and it helped to establish a sense of order in the Kievan Rus'. Volodymyr also expanded the federation's influence, establishing diplomatic ties with neighboring kingdoms and engaging in trade with Byzantium and the Islamic world.

Volodymyr's reign was marked by impressive accomplishments that helped to consolidate his power and establish the Kievan Rus' as a major power in Eastern Europe. One of his most significant accomplishments was the construction of the Saint Sophia Cathedral in Kiev. This magnificent cathedral was built to rival the great churches of Constantinople and Rome, and it served as a symbol of Kievan Rus''s power and prosperity.

One of the most significant events of Volodymyr's reign was his conversion to Christianity. In 988 AD, Volodymyr embraced Christianity and made it the official religion of Kievan Rus'. This was a momentous decision that had a profound impact on the development of Ukraine. Volodymyr's conversion to Christianity had several important consequences. It helped to unify the Kievan Rus', creating a sense of shared identity and purpose. It also established the Orthodox Church as a major force in Eastern Europe, and it helped to define Ukraine's cultural and religious identity.

Volodymyr's legacy is still felt in Ukraine

today. He is remembered as a great ruler who consolidated the power of the Kievan Rus' and established it as a major power in Eastern Europe. His conversion to Christianity helped to define Ukraine's cultural and religious identity, and it created a sense of shared purpose and identity among the people of Ukraine. Today, there are many cultural and historical sites in Ukraine that are related to Volodymyr the Great. The Saint Sophia Cathedral in Kiev, which he built, is one of the most impressive examples of his legacy. Other sites, such as the Golden Gate of Kiev and Saint Michael's Golden-Domed Monastery, also serve as reminders of his influence.

Despite his many accomplishments, Volodymyr's reign was not without controversy. Some historians have criticized him for his ruthless tactics, such as his decision to execute his brother Yaropolk. Others have questioned the true motives behind his conversion to Christianity, suggesting that it was driven more by political expediency than religious conviction. There are also controversies surrounding Volodymyr's legacy. Some nationalists have claimed him as a symbol of Ukrainian identity and independence, while others have criticized him for his role in establishing a centralized state that subjugated the various tribes of the Kievan Rus'.

Volodymyr the Great was a remarkable ruler who played a pivotal role in the development of Ukraine. His conversion to Christianity helped to define Ukraine's cultural and religious identity, and it created a sense of shared purpose and identity among the people of Ukraine. Despite the controversies surrounding his reign and legacy, there is no doubt that Volodymyr the Great was one of Ukraine's most influential rulers. His impact can still be felt in Ukraine today, and his legacy serves as a reminder of the country's rich cultural and historical heritage.

Taras Shevchenko

Taras Shevchenko, Self-Portrait with Candle, 1860

Taras Shevchenko is a name that is synonymous with Ukrainian culture and heritage. Born in 1814, Shevchenko's life, poetry, and artwork continue to inspire and influence generations of people, not just in Ukraine but around the world. As a writer, artist, and political activist, Shevchenko left a lasting legacy that has shaped and defined the modern Ukrainian identity.

Shevchenko's early life was shaped by the harsh realities of life as a serf. He was born into a peasant family, and from an early age, he was forced to work in the fields and tend to the livestock. Despite this, Shevchenko showed a keen interest in art and literature, and he spent any spare moment he had reading and drawing.

At the age of 14, Shevchenko was sold into serfdom and forced to work for a wealthy landowner. However, his talent did not go unnoticed, and he was eventually discovered by a wealthy patron who recognized his artistic abilities and helped him to gain his freedom and pursue his education.

Shevchenko's poetry and artwork are considered to be some of the most significant contributions to Ukrainian culture and literature. His poetry, which was written in Ukrainian, celebrated the beauty and richness of the Ukrainian landscape and people, and he was known for his keen sense of observation and his ability to capture the essence of Ukrainian life. Shevchenko's artwork, which included paintings, drawings, and etchings, was similarly focused on Ukrainian life and culture. He was known for his realistic and detailed depictions of Ukrainian peasants, landscapes, and historical events, and his artwork has come to be seen as a vital part of the Ukrainian artistic tradition.

Taras Shevchenko is considered to be one of the most significant figures in Ukrainian culture and literature. His poetry and artwork have come to represent the essence of Ukrainian identity, and his contributions to the Ukrainian language and literature are widely recognized. Shevchenko's work has also been instrumental in shaping the modern Ukrainian identity, and his influence can be seen in everything from the country's cultural traditions to its political and social landscape.

Shevchenko's impact on Ukrainian literature and language cannot be overstated. His poetry, which was written in Ukrainian, helped to establish the language as a legitimate and important medium for literature and art. Shevchenko's work also helped to elevate the status of Ukrainian literature and culture, which had previously been marginalized by the dominant Russian culture. Today, Ukrainian literature and language are thriving, and Shevchenko's contributions are seen as a vital part of the country's cultural heritage.

In addition to his artistic contributions, Shevchenko was also a political activist who fought for the rights of Ukrainian people. He was a vocal critic of the Russian Empire, which controlled Ukraine at the time, and his political views often landed him in trouble with the authorities. Despite this, Shevchenko continued to speak out against injustice and oppression, and his activism helped to inspire a generation of Ukrainians to fight for their rights and freedoms.

Shevchenko's legacy is commemorated in a variety of ways in Ukraine and around the world. His poetry and artwork are celebrated in museums and galleries, and his contributions to Ukrainian culture and literature are recognized through numerous awards and honors. In addition to this, Shevchenko's political activism and his role as a champion of Ukrainian rights and freedoms are celebrated by activists and politicians alike. His name and image are ubiquitous in Ukraine, and he is considered to be a national hero and icon.

Taras Shevchenko continues to play a vital role in shaping the modern Ukrainian identity. His art, poetry, and activism have helped to define and celebrate Ukrainian culture and heritage, and his contributions to Ukrainian literature and language have helped to establish the country's unique identity and voice. Today, Shevchenko's legacy is celebrated by Ukrainians of all ages and backgrounds, and his work continues to inspire and influence people around the world.

In conclusion, Taras Shevchenko's enduring legacy is a testament to the power of art, literature, and activism to shape and define a culture and identity. His contributions to Ukrainian culture and literature are widely recognized, and his influence can be seen in everything from the country's artistic traditions to its political and social landscape.

As Ukrainians continue to grapple with the challenges of the modern world, the legacy of Taras Shevchenko remains a source of inspiration and strength. His art, poetry, and activism continue to inspire and influence generations of people, and his contributions to Ukrainian culture and heritage will continue to be celebrated and cherished for generations to come.

Ivan Mazepa

In the pages of Ukrainian history, there are few figures as controversial as Ivan Mazepa. He was a man who, in his own time, was revered as a patriot and a hero by some, while others saw him as nothing more than a traitor and a turncoat. Even today, more than three centuries after his death, the debate about his legacy rages on. But who was Ivan Mazepa, and what made him such a polarizing figure?

Ivan Mazepa was born into a noble Ukrainian family in 1639. He received a Jesuit education in the Polish-Lithuanian Commonwealth, and eventually became a page in the court of King John II Casimir. After a brief stint as a soldier, he returned to Ukraine and entered the service of Hetman Petro Doroshenko. When Doroshenko was overthrown by the Russian Empire in 1665, Mazepa entered the service of the new hetman, Ivan Briukhovetsky.

Mazepa quickly rose through the ranks, becoming Briukhovetsky's closest advisor and confidant. When Briukhovetsky died in 1668, Mazepa was elected hetman of Ukraine by the Cossack Council. He quickly set about modernizing the Cossack army, introducing new tactics and weapons, and forging alliances with neighboring powers.

Mazepa's tenure as hetman was marked by both military success and political intrigue. He led successful campaigns against the Crimean Khanate and the Ottoman Empire, and negotiated treaties with Poland-Lithuania and Sweden. However, he was also accused of corruption and nepotism, and his relationship with the Russian Empire, which had installed him as hetman, was strained.

In the early years of the 18th century, the Great Northern War was raging across Europe. Russia, led by Peter the Great, was pitted against a coalition of northern powers, including Sweden, Denmark, and Norway. Mazepa saw an opportunity to break free from Russian domination and establish an independent Ukraine. In 1708, he entered into an alliance with Charles XII of Sweden, offering to provide troops, supplies, and intelligence in exchange for Swedish support for a Ukrainian state.

The alliance was controversial from the start. Many Cossacks saw it as a betrayal of their longstanding ties with Russia, and there were fears that Sweden would simply replace Russia as a new imperial power. Nevertheless, Mazepa pressed ahead, and in 1709, he joined Charles

XII at the Battle of Poltava, hoping to deliver a crushing blow to the Russian army.

The Battle of Poltava, fought on June 27, 1709, was a turning point in European history. It was the culmination of the Great Northern War, and a decisive victory for Russia over Sweden. Mazepa's role in the battle was controversial and, ultimately, disastrous. He led a contingent of Cossack troops into battle alongside the Swedes, but his forces were quickly overwhelmed by the Russian army. Charles XII was wounded and forced to flee to Turkey, while Mazepa escaped to the Ottoman Empire. The aftermath of the Battle of Poltava was catastrophic for Ukraine. The Russian Empire tightened its grip on the region, and Mazepa's dreams of an independent Ukrainian state were crushed. Mazepa died in exile in 1709, but his legacy lived on.

Mazepa is remembered today as a symbol of Ukrainian resistance to Russian imperialism. His alliance with Sweden, while ultimately unsuccessful, was a bold attempt to break free from centuries of foreign domination. He is also remembered for his contributions to Ukrainian culture, including his patronage of artists, writers, and musicians. However, Mazepa's legacy is also controversial. Some see him as a hero who fought for Ukrainian independence, while others see him as a traitor who sold out his country to foreign powers. His political and military career was marked by both successes and failures, and his true motivations and beliefs are still a matter of debate.

One of the biggest controversies surrounding Mazepa's legacy is his relationship with Russia. Some historians argue that he was a loyal subject of the Russian Empire who only turned against his benefactors when it suited his own interests. Others see him as a principled leader who was forced to choose between his loyalty to Russia and his desire for Ukrainian independence. Another controversy surrounds Mazepa's personal life. He was rumored to have had a number of romantic relationships with both men and women, which was highly unusual for a public figure in the 17th century. Some historians argue that these rumors were spread by his enemies to discredit him, while others believe that they are true.

Mazepa's story has inspired countless works of literature and art. One of the most famous is the poem "Poltava" by Alexander Pushkin, which tells the story of the Battle of Poltava from Mazepa's perspective. The poem portrays Mazepa as a tragic hero who is betrayed by his own people and forced to flee his homeland. In Ukraine, Mazepa is celebrated as a cultural icon. His portrait appears on Ukrainian currency, and there are numerous statues and monuments dedicated to him throughout the country. He is also the subject of numerous folk songs and legends, which portray him as a brave and noble leader who fought for the freedom of his people.

Despite the controversies surrounding his legacy, there is no denying the impact that Mazepa had on Ukrainian culture. As hetman, he worked tirelessly to promote education, the arts, and the Ukrainian language. He founded the first Ukrainian academy, which trained generations of scholars and artists. He also commissioned numerous works of art and literature, including the first Ukrainian translation of the Bible. Mazepa's legacy is still felt in Ukraine today. His vision of an independent Ukraine has inspired generations of Ukrainians, and his contributions to Ukrainian culture continue to be celebrated.

Ivan Mazepa was a complex and controversial figure who left an indelible mark on Ukrainian history. He was a man of contradictions, a patriot who was accused of treason, and a hero who was reviled as a traitor. His legacy is still the subject of debate and controversy, but there is no denying the impact that he had on Ukrainian culture and history. Whether he was a hero or a villain, Ivan Mazepa is a figure who will continue to fascinate and inspire Ukrainians for generations to come.

Mykhailo Hrushevsky

The name Mykhailo Hrushevsky is synonymous with the National Revival Movement in Ukraine. Known for his tireless efforts in promoting Ukrainian culture and language, Hrushevsky played an instrumental role in the country's struggle for independence. Born in the late 19th century, this Ukrainian historian, politician, and writer was a visionary who fought for the rights of his people during some of the most challenging times in the country's history. His contributions to the National Revival Movement are immeasurable, and his legacy continues to inspire Ukrainians to this day.

Mykhailo Hrushevsky was born on September 29, 1866, in the village of Ivanivka, in the Kyiv region of Ukraine. His father was a priest, and his family was deeply rooted in Ukrainian culture and traditions. As a child, Hrushevsky was interested in history and literature, and he spent much of his time reading books and studying Ukrainian folklore (Anonymous, n.d.). In 1886, he graduated from the Kyiv Theological Academy and went on to study history and philology at Kyiv University.

Hrushevsky's education gave him a deep understanding of Ukrainian history and culture, and he became an expert in the field. He was particularly interested in the history of the Ukrainian Cossacks, and his research on the subject became his life's work. In 1892, he published his first book, "The History of the Ukrainian Cossacks", which was well-received by both scholars and the general public. This book was the first of many that Hrushevsky would write on Ukrainian history, and it established him as a leading authority on the subject.

Throughout his life, Hrushevsky remained committed to promoting Ukrainian culture and language. He believed that these were essential to the identity of the Ukrainian people and that they needed to be preserved and celebrated. His work in this area would later become a central part of the National Revival Movement in Ukraine.

Hrushevsky's political career began in the early 20th century, and he quickly became one of the leading figures in the Ukrainian nationalist movement. He was a member of the Ukrainian Democratic Party, which was dedicated to promoting Ukrainian autonomy within the Russian Empire. Hrushevsky believed that Ukraine should be recognized as a separate nation with its own language, culture, and traditions.

In 1905, Hrushevsky was elected to the State Duma, the lower house of the Russian parliament. He used his position to advocate for the rights of Ukrainians and to promote their language and culture. He also worked to establish a Ukrainian university in Kyiv, which would provide a platform for the study and promotion of Ukrainian history and culture. In 1917, following the collapse of the Russian Empire, Hrushevsky became the head of the Ukrainian Central Rada, a provisional government that was established to govern

Ukraine. He worked tirelessly to establish Ukraine as an independent nation, and his efforts were instrumental in the country's struggle for independence.

The Ukrainian Revolution of 1917-1921 was a pivotal moment in the country's history, and Hrushevsky played a crucial role in the events that unfolded. As the head of the Ukrainian Central Rada, he led the fight for Ukrainian independence and worked to establish a functioning government that could govern the country.

During this time, Hrushevsky faced many challenges, including opposition from both the Bolsheviks and the White Army. However, he remained committed to the cause of Ukrainian independence and worked tirelessly to achieve it. In 1918, Ukraine declared its independence, and Hrushevsky became the first president of the newly established Ukrainian National Republic.

Despite his best efforts, however, Ukraine's independence was short-lived. The country was soon invaded by both the Bolsheviks and the Polish, and Hrushevsky was forced to flee into exile. He spent the next several years living in Prague and Vienna, where he continued to work for the cause of Ukrainian independence.

Mykhailo Hrushevsky left behind a powerful legacy that continues to inspire Ukrainians to this day. His commitment to promoting Ukrainian culture and language helped to establish a strong sense of national identity that has endured for generations. His work as a historian and writer helped to preserve the history of the Ukrainian people and to establish Ukraine as an important cultural and historical center.

Hrushevsky's impact on Ukrainian history is immeasurable. He played a crucial role in the country's struggle for independence, and his efforts helped to establish Ukraine as a separate nation with its own language, culture, and traditions. His work as a historian and writer helped to establish the study of Ukrainian history as a legitimate field of study, and his contributions to the field continue to be studied and admired to this day.

Throughout his life, Mykhailo Hrushevsky wrote extensively on Ukrainian history and culture. His books and articles are regarded as some of the most important works in the field, and they continue to be studied and admired to this day. Hrushevsky's most famous work is his multi-volume "History of Ukraine-Rus", which he began writing in the early 20th century. This book traces the history of Ukraine from ancient times to the present day and is considered to be one of the most comprehensive works on Ukrainian history ever written. Hrushevsky's other notable works include "The History of the Ukrainian Cossacks", "The Ukrainian Revolution", and "The History of Ukraine".

Mykhailo Hrushevsky is revered in modern Ukraine as a hero and a patriot. His contributions to Ukrainian culture and history are celebrated every year on his birthday, September 29th. In Kyiv, a statue of Hrushevsky stands in the center of the city, and there are many streets, buildings, and institutions named after him. Hrushevsky's legacy is also celebrated in the arts. Many Ukrainian musicians, writers, and artists have paid tribute to him in their work, and his life and contributions have been the subject of numerous films, plays, and other artistic works.

Despite his many contributions to Ukrainian history and culture, Mykhailo Hrushevsky has not been without his critics. Some have accused him of being too focused on Ukrainian nationalism, to the exclusion of other cultures and traditions. Others have criticized his work as a historian, arguing that he was biased in his interpretation of Ukrainian history. Still, others have criticized Hrushevsky's political career, arguing that he was too willing to work with other nationalist groups, even if they did not share his vision for Ukraine. Despite these criticisms, however, Hrushevsky's contributions to Ukrainian history and culture remain widely recognized and celebrated.

Mykhailo Hrushevsky remains an important figure in Ukrainian history and culture, and his legacy continues to inspire Ukrainians to this day. His work as a historian and writer has helped to preserve the history and culture of the Ukrainian people, and his contributions to the National Revival Movement have helped to establish Ukraine as a separate nation with its own language, culture, and traditions. In today's Ukraine, Hrushevsky's legacy continues to be celebrated and studied. His works remain important sources of information and inspiration for scholars and students alike, and his impact on Ukrainian history and culture continues to be felt.

Mykhailo Hrushevsky was a visionary who fought tirelessly for the rights of the Ukrainian people. His contributions to the National Revival Movement in Ukraine are immeasurable, and his legacy continues to inspire Ukrainians to this day. As a historian, politician, and writer, Hrushevsky left behind a powerful legacy that has helped to shape the course of Ukrainian history and culture. His commitment to promoting Ukrainian language and culture, and his work as a historian, has helped to establish Ukraine as an important cultural and historical center. Today, Hrushevsky remains an important figure in Ukrainian history and culture, and his legacy continues to be celebrated and studied.

Stepan Bandera

Stepan Bandera was a complex and controversial figure, whose life and legacy have been debated for decades. Born in 1909 in the Austro-Hungarian province of Galicia, Bandera came of age during a tumultuous period in Ukrainian history. At the time, Ukraine was divided between various empires and powers, and many Ukrainians were agitating for independence and self-determination. Bandera was drawn to this cause from an early age, and he soon became involved in various nationalist groups and organizations.

Bandera's family was deeply involved in Ukrainian politics and culture. His father was a Greek-Catholic priest, and his mother was a teacher and activist. From a young age, Bandera was exposed to Ukrainian culture and language, and he quickly became passionate about the idea of a free and independent Ukraine. As a teenager, he joined the Ukrainian Youth Association, a nationalist organization that aimed to promote Ukrainian culture and language.

In the early 1930s, Bandera became involved in the Organization of Ukrainian Nationalists (OUN), a radical nationalist group that aimed to achieve Ukrainian independence through armed struggle. Bandera quickly rose through the ranks of the organization, becoming one of its most prominent leaders. He was known for his charisma, intelligence, and unwavering dedication to the cause of Ukrainian nationalism.

The OUN was founded in 1929, and it quickly became one of the most prominent nationalist groups in Ukraine. The organization was committed to achieving Ukrainian independence through any means necessary, including armed struggle. The OUN was highly secretive and hierarchical, with a small group of leaders at the top who controlled the organization's activities. Bandera quickly rose through the ranks of the OUN, becoming one of its most prominent leaders. Bandera believed that Ukraine had a right to independence and self-determination, and he was willing to do whatever it took to achieve those goals.

In 1934, Bandera was arrested by Polish authorities and imprisoned for his involvement in the OUN. He spent the next several years in prison, where he was subjected to harsh conditions and torture. Despite this, Bandera remained committed to the cause of Ukrainian independence, and he continued to work with the OUN from behind bars. In 1939, Bandera was released from prison and exiled to Germany, where he continued to work with the OUN. During this time, Bandera became increasingly radicalized, and he began to embrace more extreme tactics in his fight for Ukrainian independence.

During World War II, Bandera and the OUN aligned themselves with Nazi Germany, believing that the Germans would help them achieve Ukrainian independence. Bandera saw the war as an opportunity to strike a blow against the Soviet Union, which he saw as the main obstacle to Ukrainian independence. Bandera and the OUN formed a Ukrainian national army, known as the Ukrainian Insurgent Army (UIA), which fought against both the Germans and the Soviets. The UIA engaged in guerrilla warfare, sabotage, and assassinations, targeting both German and Soviet forces as well as Ukrainian collaborators.

Bandera and the OUN's alliance with Nazi Germany has been a source of controversy and debate for decades. Some see it as a necessary tactic in the fight for Ukrainian independence, while others see it as a betrayal of Ukrainian values and an endorsement of Nazi ideology. Bandera's association with the UIA, which committed a number of atrocities during the war, has also been a subject of controversy. The UIA was responsible for the deaths of tens of thousands of people, including Jews, Poles, and Ukrainians who were seen as collaborators.

Despite the controversies surrounding Bandera and the OUN, there is no denying that they played a significant role in the history of Ukrainian nationalism and independence.

Bandera and the OUN helped to keep the idea of Ukrainian independence alive during a period when it seemed impossible. They inspired a new generation of Ukrainian nationalists, who would go on to play a key role in the country's eventual independence in 1991. Today, Bandera is seen by many Ukrainians as a national hero, who fought for his country's freedom and independence. He is celebrated in Ukraine as a symbol of resistance against foreign oppression and a champion of Ukrainian values and culture.

In modern-day Ukraine, Bandera's legacy is still very much alive despite it being the subject of intense debate and controversy, both within Ukraine and internationally. He was a dedicated nationalist who fought tirelessly for Ukrainian independence and self-determination, but his association with Nazi Germany and the UIA's atrocities had cast a shadow over his legacy. Many accused him of collaborating with Nazi Germany and committing atrocities during World War II, while others saw him as a hero who fought against impossible odds for his country's freedom and independence. The controversy surrounding Bandera's legacy highlights the complex and often painful history of Ukraine and its struggle for independence. It also underscores the importance of understanding the historical context and forces that shaped Bandera's life and legacy.

Despite the controversies surrounding Bandera and the OUN, there is no denying that they played a significant role in the history of Ukrainian nationalism and independence. Today, Bandera is celebrated by many Ukrainians as a symbol of resistance against foreign oppression and a champion of Ukrainian values and culture. As Ukraine continues to grapple with the legacy of its past, the story of Stepan Bandera serves as a reminder of the complex and often painful history of the country and its people. It is a story that deserves to be told and understood, so that future generations can learn from the mistakes of the past and build a better future for themselves and their country. There are numerous monuments, streets, and buildings named after him throughout the country, and he is celebrated every year on January 1st, which is his birthday.

Viktor Yushchenko

The political arena is a dynamic and ever-changing landscape that often leads to surprising outcomes. One such journey is that of Viktor Yushchenko, a Ukrainian politician who rose to power on the back of the Orange Revolution in 2004. Yushchenko's tenure as the President of Ukraine was marked by a series of dramatic events that transformed the country's political landscape. From his pro-Western policies to his bitter feud with his former ally, Yulia Tymoshenko, Yushchenko's journey was filled with twists and turns. However, despite his initial popularity, Yushchenko's tenure was not without its controversies, and his eventual fall from power was as swift as it was unexpected.

Viktor Yushchenko's political career began in the early 1990s when he was appointed as the governor of the National Bank of Ukraine. He was later appointed as the Prime Minister of Ukraine in 1999 by then-President Leonid Kuchma. However, Yushchenko's tenure as the Prime Minister was short-lived, and he was removed from office in 2001 after a vote of no-confidence.

Despite this setback, Yushchenko continued to be active in politics and emerged as the leader of the opposition to the Kuchma regime. In 2004, he ran for the presidency of Ukraine against Kuchma's hand-picked successor, Viktor Yanukovych. The election was marred by allegations of fraud, and Yushchenko's supporters launched a series of protests that became known as the Orange Revolution. The protests eventually forced a rerun of the election, which Yushchenko won in December 2004.

The presidential campaign of 2004 was one of the most contentious in Ukraine's history. Yushchenko's main opponent, Viktor Yanukovych, was supported by the establishment and the Russian government. Yushchenko, on the other hand, was seen as a pro-Western candidate who would steer Ukraine towards closer ties with Europe. The election was marred by allegations of fraud, with Yanukovych being declared the winner.

However, Yushchenko and his supporters launched a series of protests that became known as the Orange Revolution. The protests were peaceful and involved thousands of Ukrainians who gathered in the streets of Kiev to demand a free and fair election. The protests eventually forced a rerun of the election, which was overseen by international observers. Yushchenko won the rerun with over 50% of the vote, and he was inaugurated as the President of Ukraine on January 23, 2005.

As the President of Ukraine, Viktor Yushchenko implemented a series of reforms aimed at modernizing the country's economy and political system. He pursued a pro-Western foreign policy, seeking closer ties with the European Union and the United States. Yushchenko also implemented economic reforms aimed at reducing corruption and increasing foreign investment in Ukraine. He introduced a flat tax system and implemented measures to improve the business climate in the country. Additionally, he pursued reforms aimed at decentralizing power in Ukraine, giving more autonomy to local governments.

Despite his initial popularity, Yushchenko's presidency was not without its controversies. One of the most significant challenges he faced was his bitter feud with his former ally, Yulia Tymoshenko. Tymoshenko was appointed as the Prime Minister of Ukraine in 2005, but she and Yushchenko quickly became embroiled in a power struggle. The feud between Yushchenko and Tymoshenko led to political instability in Ukraine, with the government being unable to pass significant reforms. Additionally, Yushchenko's pro-Western policies were met with resistance from Russia, which saw Ukraine's move towards the West as a threat to its own interests.

Yushchenko's decline in popularity began in 2006 when he dismissed Tymoshenko as Prime Minister. The move was widely seen as an abuse of power, and Yushchenko's approval ratings began to plummet. Additionally, his government was seen as ineffective, with corruption remaining a significant problem in Ukraine. Yushchenko's popularity continued to decline, and he was defeated in the 2010 presidential election by Viktor Yanukovych, his former opponent in the 2004 election. Yushchenko received only 5.5% of the vote, a significant drop from the over 50% he received in 2004.

Despite his eventual fall from power, Viktor Yushchenko's presidency had a significant impact on Ukraine's politics and society. His pro-Western policies paved the way for closer ties with Europe and the United States, and he implemented significant reforms aimed at modernizing Ukraine's economy and political system. However, Yushchenko's presidency was also marked by political instability and a bitter feud with his former ally, Yulia Tymoshenko. Additionally, his decline in popularity and defeat in the 2010 election highlighted the challenges of implementing significant reforms in a politically divided country like Ukraine.

The political journey of Viktor Yushchenko provides valuable lessons for leaders and policymakers around the world. One of the most significant lessons is the importance of a unified government in implementing significant reforms. Yushchenko's bitter feud with Tymoshenko highlights the challenges of implementing reforms in a politically divided country. Additionally, Yushchenko's presidency highlights the importance of balancing domestic and foreign policy goals. His pro-Western policies were met with resistance from Russia, highlighting the challenges of pursuing a foreign policy that may be at odds with the interests of a powerful neighbor.

Viktor Yushchenko's political journey was a

rollercoaster ride through the turbulent world of Ukrainian politics. From his rise to power on the back of the Orange Revolution to his bitter feud with his former ally, Yulia Tymoshenko, Yushchenko's tenure as the President of Ukraine was marked by a series of dramatic events that transformed the country's political landscape.

Despite his initial popularity, Yushchenko's presidency was not without its controversies, and his eventual fall from power was as swift as it was unexpected. However, his presidency had a significant impact on Ukraine's politics and society, paving the way for closer ties with Europe and the United States and implementing significant reforms aimed at modernizing Ukraine's economy and political system.

The lessons learned from Yushchenko's political journey provide valuable insights for leaders and policymakers around the world, highlighting the challenges of implementing significant reforms in a politically divided country and the importance of balancing domestic and foreign policy goals.

Petro Poroshenko

Over the past five years, Petro Poroshenko served as the President of Ukraine and faced the daunting task of leading a country through a challenging period in its history. From the annexation of Crimea by Russia to the ongoing conflict in the Donbass region, Poroshenko's presidency was marked by constant political turbulence and economic hardship. Now, as his term has come to an end, it's time to take a critical look at his legacy and assess the impact of his policies on the country.

Petro Poroshenko was elected as the President of Ukraine in 2014, following the Euromaidan protests that led to the ousting of Viktor Yanukovych. Poroshenko's presidency was marked by constant political turbulence and economic hardship, as Ukraine faced a number of challenges both domestically and internationally. One of Poroshenko's primary goals as president was to strengthen Ukraine's ties with the West and move the country closer towards European integration. He was successful in securing a number of agreements with the European Union, including a visa-free travel regime and an association agreement. However, he faced significant opposition from Russia, which annexed Crimea from Ukraine in 2014 and backed separatist rebels in the Donbass region.

Poroshenko's economic policies were aimed at stabilizing Ukraine's economy and attracting foreign investment. His government implemented a number of reforms, including pension and tax reforms, and increased efforts to combat corruption. While these reforms were necessary, they also had a significant impact on the Ukrainian population. The pension reforms, for example, led to a significant increase in the retirement age and a reduction in benefits. The tax reforms, meanwhile, increased the tax burden on small businesses and entrepreneurs.

Poroshenko's presidency was marked by a number of political controversies and challenges. One of the most significant was his handling of corruption allegations, which many accused him of not doing enough to address. His government was also criticized for its slow progress in implementing reforms, and for the continued influence of oligarchs in Ukrainian politics. Poroshenko himself was accused of having ties to oligarchs and of using his position for personal gain.

Poroshenko's foreign policy was largely focused on moving Ukraine closer towards the West and away from Russia. He was a vocal critic of Russian aggression in Ukraine and called for increased support from the international community. However, his efforts to distance Ukraine from Russia were met with resistance from Moscow, which imposed economic sanctions on Ukraine and backed separatist rebels in the Donbass region. Poroshenko's government also faced criticism from some Ukrainians who believed that he was not doing enough to resolve the conflict with Russia.

The ongoing conflict between Ukraine and Russia was a major challenge for Poroshenko's presidency. His government was forced to deal with separatist rebels in the Donbass region, as well as Russian military intervention in the conflict. Poroshenko's government implemented a number of measures to combat the conflict, including a ceasefire and the creation of a new police force in the Donbass region. However, these efforts were met with mixed results, and the conflict continued to simmer throughout his presidency.

Poroshenko's leadership style was marked by a strong focus on national unity and a commitment to Ukraine's European integration. He was seen as a decisive leader who was willing to take bold actions to protect Ukraine's sovereignty. However, his leadership was also criticized for being too focused on his own personal interests, and for not doing enough to address corruption and oligarchic influence in Ukrainian politics. Some also believed that he was too willing to compromise with Russia and that he did not take a strong enough stance against Russian aggression.

Poroshenko's presidency was marked by a number of similarities to previous Ukrainian leaders, including a focus on national unity and a commitment to European integration. However, his government also faced many of the same challenges as previous leaders, including corruption, oligarchic influence, and conflict with Russia. Despite these challenges, Poroshenko was seen by many as a more decisive leader than his predecessors. He was willing to take bold actions to protect Ukraine's sovereignty and was vocal in his opposition to Russian aggression.

The legacy of Poroshenko's presidency is complex and multifaceted. While he made progress in a number of areas, including economic reforms and European integration, his government also faced significant challenges and controversies. Poroshenko will be remembered for his efforts to move Ukraine closer towards the West and for his strong stance against Russian aggression. However, his presidency was also marked by accusations of corruption and oligarchic influence, and his government faced criticism for its slow progress in implementing reforms.

Petro Poroshenko's presidency was marked by both successes and failures. His government made progress in a number of areas, including economic reforms and European integration, but also faced significant challenges and controversies. Ultimately, Poroshenko's impact on Ukraine's future remains to be seen. While he took important steps towards strengthening Ukraine's ties with the West, the country still faces significant challenges, including corruption, conflict with Russia, and economic instability. Only time will tell how Poroshenko's legacy will shape Ukraine's future.

A Timeline of the Major Events in the Political History of Ukraine Since It Became Independent From Russia in 1991

1991 – The leader of the Soviet Republic of Ukraine, Leonid Kravchuk, declared independence from Russia. In a presidential election and referendum, Ukrainians approved independence and elected Kravchuk as president.

1994 – Kravchuk loses to Leonid Kuchma in a free and fair presidential election.

1999 – In elections largely riddled with indiscretions, Kuchma is re-elected.

2004 – Victor Yanukovich, a pro-Russian candidate, is announced as president but protests that become known as the Orange Revolution are triggered by assertions of vote rigging. This forces a rerun of the elections. Viktor Yushchenko, a pro-Western former prime minister, is voted in as president.

2005 – Yushchenko becomes president and promises Ukrainians to lead the country out of the Kremlin's orbit, towards the EU and NATO. He assigns Yulia Tymoshenko, a former executive of an energy company as Prime Minister; however, after a bitter rivalry within the pro-Western camp, she is fired.

2008 – NATO makes a promise to Ukraine that one day it will join the coalition.

2010 – Tymoshenko loses to Yanukovich at the presidential elections. Ukraine and Russia agree to a gas pricing treaty in return for an extended lease for Russia's navy in Ukraine's Black Sea port.

2013 – In November, Yanukovich's administration suspended association negotiations and trade with the EU. They opt to re-establish economic ties with Russia, causing months-long mass protests in Kyiv.

2014 – The protests that take place mainly around Kiev's Maidan square become violent and masses of protesters are slain.

February 2014 – The parliament decides to remove Yanukovich as president. He later flees. In a matter of days, parliament in Crimea, a region in Ukraine, is seized by armed men who also raise Russia's flag. After the March 16 referendum, Moscow extended the territory, which demonstrates overpowering support in Crimea for being a member of the Russian Federation.

April 2014 – The declaration of independence by Pro-Russian separatists in the Donbass region of eastern Ukraine led to the outbreak of fights, which has persisted intermittently until

2022, despite numerous attempts at ceasefires.

May 2014 – Petro Poroshenko, who is a politician and businessperson, became president with an agenda of the pro-Western camp.

July 2014 – A missile brought down MH17, a passenger plane flying from Amsterdam to Kuala Lumpur. All 298 passengers who were on board the plane were killed. Investigators linked the weaponry that was utilized to Russia. Russia denied its involvement.

2017 – An association treaty between the EU and Ukraine opened the free trading of services and goods on the markets, and visa-free traveling for Ukrainians to the EU.

2019 – In Ukraine, a newly established Orthodox Church was officially acknowledged, causing frustration for the Kremlin. In April's presidential election, former actor and comedian Volodymyr Zelenskiy won against Poroshenko by vowing to combat corruption and end the conflict in eastern Ukraine. In July, Zelenskiy's political party, 'Servant of the People', won in the parliamentary election. During the same month, U.S. President Donald Trump requested Zelenskiy to investigate Joe Biden, his competitor in the U.S. presidential race, and Biden's son, Hunter, for possible business connections in Ukraine. The call ultimately led to an unsuccessful attempt to impeach Donald Trump.

March 2020 – In order to curb COVID-19, Ukraine went into its first lockdown.

June 2020 – The IMF approved a $5 billion financial rescue to assist Ukraine to survive a recession that was induced by COVID-19.

January 2021 – Zelenskiy appealed to U.S. president, Joe Biden, to allow Ukraine to become a member of NATO (North Atlantic Treaty Organization).

February 2021 – Zelenskiy's administration enforced sanctions on Kremlin's very important associate in Ukraine and leader of the opposition, Viktor Medvedchuk.

Spring 2021 – Russia places a huge number of armed forces near the borders of Ukraine and says it's just a drill.

October 2021 – Ukraine angered Russia by using, for the first time in Eastern Ukraine, a Turkish Bayraktar TB2 drone.

Autumn 2021 – Russia started placing armed forces again near Ukraine's borders

December 7, 2021 – Biden warned Russia that they would extend Western economic sanctions if they invade Ukraine.

December 17 – Russia presented thorough security demands that included a lawfully binding agreement that NATO would give up any military action in Ukraine and in the East of Europe.

January 14 – Ukraine's government websites were hit by a cyber-attack warning them to "be afraid and expect the worst".

January 17 – Russian militaries started arriving in the North of Ukraine (Belarus), for joint military exercises.

January 24 – NATO placed militaries as backup and reinforced Eastern Europe with more fighter jets and ships.

January 26 – Washington responded in writing to Russia about the security demand that they made–they repeated a pledge to NATO's "open-door" approach while presenting "pragmatic" deliberations of Moscow's apprehensions.

January 28 – Russia's President, Vladimir Putin, said his country's key security demands had not been given the necessary attention.

February 2 – The United States said it would send an extra 3,000 armed forces to Romania and Poland to assist in shielding NATO associates in Eastern Europe so that the invasion does not affect them.

February 4 – At the Beijing Winter Olympics, Putin won the support of China when he demanded that Ukraine not be permitted to become a member of NATO.

February 7 – Emmanuel Macron, French

President, was hopeful that the crisis would be resolved diplomatically after he met in the Kremlin with Putin. Macron then visited Kyiv and praised Zelenskiy and the people of Ukraine for the "sang-froid".

February 9 – The U.S. State Department urged Americans living in Ukraine to leave the country as soon as possible as Biden said "things could go crazy quickly". Other nations also urged their citizens to leave Ukraine immediately.

February 14 – Zelenskiy urged Ukrainians to sing in unison Ukraine's national anthem and fly the country's flag on Feb 16, a day that was announced by some Western media houses as the day that Russia could possibly invade Ukraine.

February 15 – Russia announced that some of its armed forces would be going back to their base after their military exercises close to Ukraine's borders. Russia mocked the West about their forewarnings about an imminent invasion. The parliament in Russia asked Putin to acknowledge two Russian-backed breakaway states in Eastern Ukraine as being independent states.

February 18 – Michael Carpenter, U.S. ambassador to the Organization for Security and Cooperation, said possibilities are Russia has placed between 169,000- 190,000 armed forces in and close to Ukraine.

February 19 – Russia's tactical nuclear militaries held military exercises supervised by Putin.

February 21 – Macron said Putin and Biden principally agreed to hold talks over Ukraine. In an address on television, Putin said Ukraine is a vital part of Russia's history, the nation has never had a stable government, foreign powers are at the country's forefront, and it has a puppet government. Putin signed agreements to acknowledge sovereign states in the East of Ukraine as being independent and sent Russian militaries there.

February 22 – The UK, U.S., and their associates enacted sanctions on Russia's members of parliament, financial institutions, and other possessions. Germany halted the approval of the final accreditation of the Nord Stream 2 pipeline. In a television address, Putin made demands that Ukraine withdraw its armed forces and said the Minsk peace deal over autonomous states was no longer in place. He blamed Kyiv for ending the deal.

February 23 – Separatist leaders who were backed by Russia asked Russia to assist them in preventing violence from the Ukrainian military.

February 24 – Russia's head of State, Vladimir

Putin authorized "special military operations" in the East of Ukraine, and in a televised address, he asked Ukrainian militaries to put down their weaponries. Russian militaries began artillery and missile attacks on Ukraine's air bases and forces, which struck regions in big cities.

REFERENCES

Anonymous. (2017). Ukraine in the Flames of the 1917 Revolution. Retrieved from https://huri.harvard.edu/nes/ukraine-flames-1917-revolution

Anonymous. (2021). Stepan Bandera - leader of the Organisation of Ukrainian Nationalists. Retrieved from https://ipn.gov.pl/en/digital-resources/articles/8044,Stepan-Bandera-leader-of-the-Organisation-of-Ukrainian-Nationalists.html

Anonymous. (2022). A Ukrainian Cossack Hetman Accirding to Russian Archival Sources: Ivan Stepanovich Mazepa (1639-1709). Retrieved from https://iupress.istanbul.edu.tr/en/journal/jses/article/rus-arsiv-kaynaklarina-gore-bir-ukrayna-kazak-hetman-ivan-stepanovic-mazepa-1639-1709

Anonymous. (2023). Kievan Rus'. Retrieved from https://www.britannica.com/topic/Kyivan-Rus

Anonymous. (2023). Viktor Yushchenko - president of Ukraine. Retrieved from https://www.britannica.com/biography/Viktor-Yushchenko

Anonymous. (n.d.). Kiev during the state of Prince Volodymyr the Great. The Introduction of Christianity as state religion. Retrieved from https://geomap.com.ua/en-uh7/296.html

Anonymous. (n.d.). Petro Poroshenko - President of Ukraine. Retreved from https://www.britannica.com/biography/Petro-Poroshenko

Anonymous. (n.d.). Political Culture of Cossack Ukraine. Retrieved from https://www.ualberta.ca/canadian-institute-of-ukrainian-studies/centres-and-programs/jacyk-centre/political-culture-of-cossack-ukraine.html

Anonymous. (n.d.). Tara Shevchenko Biography.

Retrieved from https://shevchenko.ca/taras-shevchenko/biography/

Anonymous. (n.d.). Ukraine. Retrieved from https://www.britannica.com/place/Ukraine

Anonymous. (n.d.). War in Ukraine - The Policy Challenge. Retrieved from https://www.oecd.org/ukraine-hub/en/

Anonymous. (n.d.). Who was Mykhailo Hrushevsky. Retrieved from https://www,ualberta.ca/canadian-institute-of-ukrainian-studies/centres-and-programs/jacyk-centre/hrushevsky-translation-project/who-was-mykhailo-hrushevsky.html

Aqaoglu, L. (2022). A History of Ukraine. RadioLemberg. Retrieved from https://www.radiolemberg.com/en/ua-articles/ua-allarticles/a-history-of-ukraine-episode-8-great-victories-of-great-scythia

Artist, U. (2021, November 11). Portrait of Ivan Mazepa. World History Encyclopedia. Retrieved from https://www.worldhistory.org/image/14821/portrait-of-ivan-mazepa/

Cartwright. M. (2019). The Mongol Invasion of Europe. World History Encyclopedia. Retrieved from https://www.worldhistory.org/article/1453/the-mongol-invasion-of-europe/

Flier, M.S., and Graziosi, A. (2017). The Battle for Ukrainian: An Introduction. Harvard Ukrainian Studies. Retrieved from https://www.husj.harvard.edu/articles/the-battle-for-ukranian-an-introduction

Greenspan, J., (2022). Ukraine Has Seen Centuries of Conflict. History.com. Retrieved from https://www.history.com/news/ukraine-timeline-invasions

Rzeczycki, M. (n.d.). The Union of Lublin - The Origins of Republican Political Space. Polish History. Retrieved from https://polishhistory.pl/the-union-of-lublin-republican-political-space/

Wolczuk, K. (2001). Chapter two. In search of a tradition:

discontinuities of statehood in Ukraine's history. In The Moulding of Ukraine: The Constitutional Politics of State Formation. Central European University Press. Retrieved from http://books.openedition.org/ceup/1739

FREE BONUS FROM HBA: EBOOK BUNDLE

Greetings!

First of all, thank you for reading our books. As fellow passionate readers of History and Mythology, we aim to create the very best books for our readers.

Now, we invite you to join our VIP list. As a welcome gift, we offer the History & Mythology Ebook Bundle below for free. Plus you can be the first to receive new books and exclusives! Remember it's 100% free to join.

Simply scan the QR code to join.

OTHER BOOKS BY
HISTORY BROUGHT ALIVE

Available now in Ebook, Paperback, Hardcover,
and Audiobook in all regions.

For Kids:

UKRAINE HISTORY

We sincerely hope you enjoyed our new book *"Ukraine History"*. We would greatly appreciate your feedback with an honest review at the place of purchase.

First and foremost, we are always looking to grow and improve as a team. It is reassuring to hear what works, as well as receive constructive feedback on what should improve. Second, starting out as an unknown author is exceedingly difficult, and Amazon reviews go a long way toward making the journey out of anonymity possible. Please take a few minutes to write an honest review.

Best regards,
History Brought Alive
http://historybroughtalive.com/

Printed in Great Britain
by Amazon